Move Beyond intro A

TEACHER'S EDITION PACK

macmillan education

Anna Cole
David Corp
Alexandra Hearn

AT THE PARTY

Grammar (2): *Be*: negative, questions, and short answers; question words

Vocabulary (2): Numbers 20–100, days of the week, months; phone contacts

LISTENING & VOCABULARY	GRAMMAR (2)	LANGUAGE & BEYOND	SPEAKING	WRITING
It's a small world! ***Listen to a description of where things are from*** **Vocabulary (2):** Countries and nationalities	*This/that, these/those* ***Talk about the things around you***	School skills ***Be a good classmate***	Is it new? ***Describe things***	My things (description) ***Write a description of a thing***
Whose is it? ***Listen to a quiz show*** **Vocabulary (2):** Parts of the body	*Whose?*; possessive *'s/s'* and possessive pronouns ***Talk about your things, family, and friends***	School skills ***Be friendly to other students***	On the phone ***Talk on the phone***	My favorite person (description) ***Write a description of a person***
A new neighbor ***Listen to a description of a room*** **Vocabulary (2):** Things in your room	*There is / there are* ***Describe a room***	School skills ***Prepare your things for school***	You're welcome ***Ask for and give things***	Don't forget (note) ***Write a note***
Are you musical? ***Listen to street interviews*** PRONOUNCE The /v/ sound **Vocabulary (2):** Music	Simple present ***Talk about habits and routines***	School skills ***Write down your homework***	What time is it? ***Tell the time***	My free time (email) ***Write an email***

CONTENTS

WELCOME TO THE *MOVE BEYOND* TEACHER'S EDITION

Move Beyond is an exciting eight-level course for teenagers, covering CEFR levels from A1+ to B2. Its scope and sequence is meticulously mapped to the CEFR and international exams. The course offers comprehensive coverage of the four language skills through the incremental and cumulative development of subskills. It equips students with transferable linguistic strategies to use in the English classroom and beyond. The inclusion of age-appropriate 21st-century skills adds an inspiring new dimension to language teaching. The school skills lessons create a learning environment that is relevant and accessible to teenagers.

The course is flexible and works in a number of teaching contexts. Lessons are clearly labeled so that you can choose to prioritize material that's relevant in your teaching contexts. The extensive online materials present you with a variety of teaching and practice alternatives to enrich the learning experience.

With eight levels, your school's needs can be met with one single course – be it for streaming, multilevel entry or a program that takes your students from A1+ all the way up to B2.

The material has a creative and dynamic approach to topics that motivates students and makes language learning more meaningful and successful. Units provide constant opportunities for students to express themselves, while the pages are brought to life through a series of specially produced videos. Throughout the course, language is recycled and reviewed, allowing students to assess and consolidate their progress.

The combination of language skills, life skills, and motivating material in *Move Beyond* prepares students for success in and beyond the classroom.

A message from the authors

Secondary teaching is a rewarding but demanding profession. With this course we have tried to make your role as a teacher as easy as possible. The material is clearly organized and can be taught with little or no preparation time. We have also provided resources to help you test and evaluate progress, review material, and work with mixed-ability classes.

Having enthusiastic and interested students also makes the teaching role easier, so throughout the creation of this series we have considered the teenagers' perspective on learning and come up with materials that teach them about the world and allow them to express their views of the world.

When producing the course we used the following key principles to guide our writing.

10 KEY PRINCIPLES OF *MOVE BEYOND*

1 Subskills: learning how to read, listen, speak, and write

All reading, listening, speaking, and writing lessons have an integrated subskills focus that teaches students linguistic strategies to maximize their learning. This comprehensive subskills syllabus is a key part of the literacy development objective of *Move Beyond*.

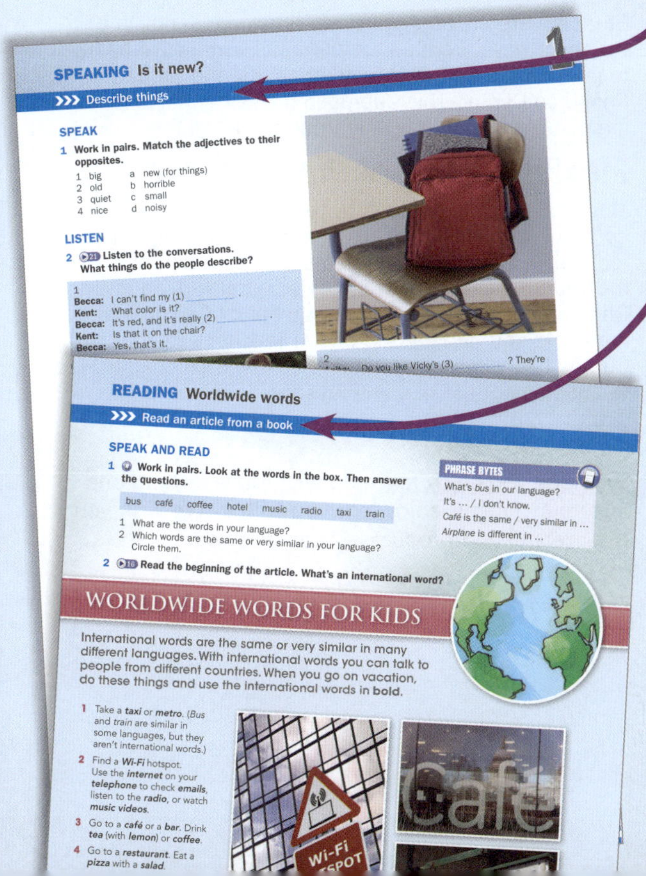

2 School skills: learning to learn

To be successful at school (and later on in life), students need to learn skills that go beyond pure academic knowledge. At the beginning of secondary school, it is imperative that students consolidate basic social and organizational skills such as being a good classmate, organizing school supplies, and doing homework. One lesson in every unit is dedicated to developing a school skill in order to help students cope in the classroom and to give them a good foundation for learning for life.

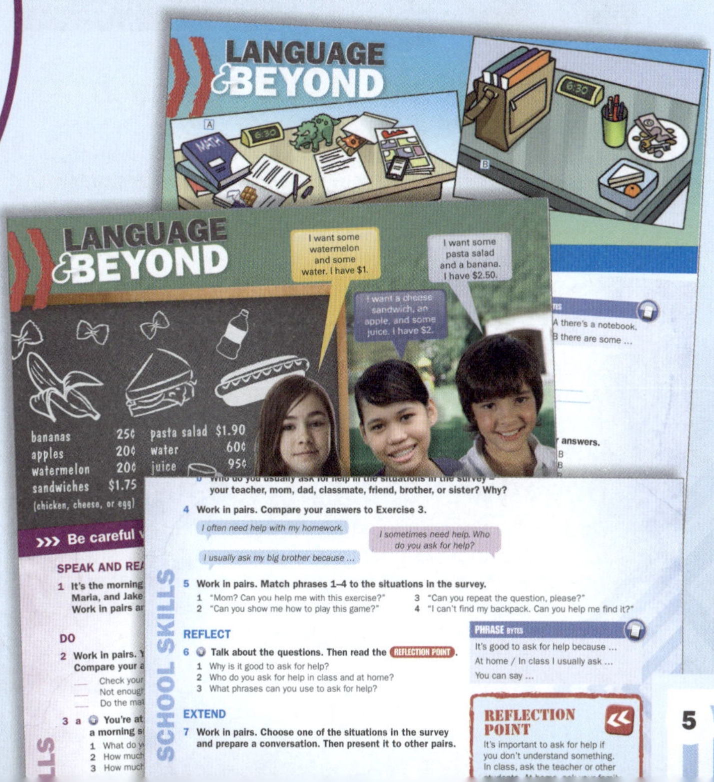

3 Original content and striking images

The cross-curricular focus of *Move Beyond* helps students learn about the world around them. The original material sustains students' interest. The striking images create a strong visual impact and engage students with the content.

4 Varied and adaptable approach

Move Beyond provides adaptations for students' differing learning styles and levels. There are ideas and prompts for students who need more help and a varied approach to dealing with topics and language. To help with differentiation in the classroom, the Teacher's Edition suggests alternative procedures for more confident or less confident students and for fast finishers.

5 Clear and easy to use

All lessons in *Move Beyond* are easy to teach directly from the page. Goals and stages are clearly marked so that teachers can quickly see the objectives and structure of each lesson.

6 Opportunities for personalization

Throughout the course, students are encouraged to relate what they have learned to their own experiences. This personal investment in the course is motivating and rewarding, and it makes the learning process more memorable and the content more relevant.

7 Strong communication focus

In *Move Beyond*, the pairwork discussions, functional speaking tasks, presentations, and variety of writing tasks all encourage students to produce meaningful and real communication.

8 Language in context

All new language in *Move Beyond* is contextualized so that students can see its function and form in realistic situations before studying the grammar rules.

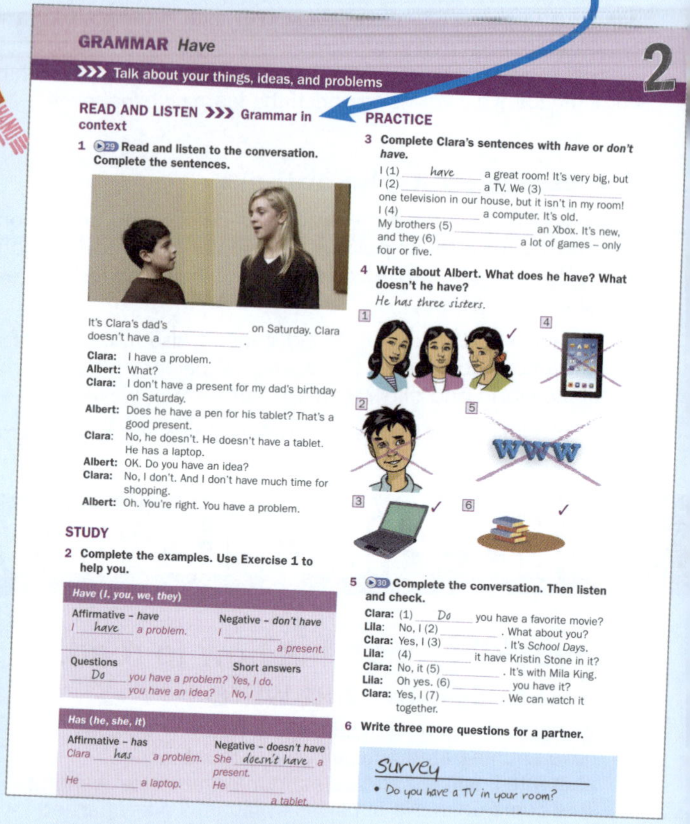

GRAMMAR *Have* 2

››› Talk about your things, ideas, and problems

READ AND LISTEN ››› Grammar in context

1 **(29) Read and listen to the conversation. Complete the sentences.**

It's Clara's dad's ________ on Saturday. Clara doesn't have a ________.

Clara: I have a problem.
Albert: What?
Clara: I don't have a present for my dad's birthday on Saturday.
Albert: Does he have a pen for his tablet? That's a good present.
Clara: No, he doesn't. He doesn't have a tablet. He has a laptop.
Albert: OK. Do you have an idea?
Clara: No, I don't. And I don't have much time for shopping.
Albert: Oh. You're right. You have a problem.

STUDY

2 **Complete the examples. Use Exercise 1 to help you.**

Have (I, you, we, they)	
Affirmative – *have* I __have__ a problem.	Negative – *don't have* I ________ a present.
Questions __Do__ you have a problem? ________ you have an idea?	Short answers Yes, I do. No, I ________.

Has (he, she, it)	
Affirmative – *has* Clara __has__ a problem. He ________ a laptop.	Negative – *doesn't have* She __doesn't have__ a present. He ________ a tablet.

PRACTICE

3 **Complete Clara's sentences with *have* or *don't have*.**

I (1) __have__ a great room! It's very big, but I (2) ________ a TV. We (3) ________ one television in our house, but it isn't in my room! I (4) ________ a computer. It's old. My brothers (5) ________ an Xbox. It's new, and they (6) ________ a lot of games – only four or five.

4 **Write about Albert. What does he have? What doesn't he have?**

He has three sisters.

1 2 3 4 5 6

5 **(30) Complete the conversation. Then listen and check.**

Clara: (1) __Do__ you have a favorite movie?
Lila: No, I (2) ________. What about you?
Clara: Yes, I (3) ________. It's *School Days*.
Lila: (4) ________ it have Kristin Stone in it?
Clara: No, it (5) ________. It's with Mila King.
Lila: Oh yes. (6) ________ you have it?
Clara: Yes, I (7) ________. We can watch it together.

6 **Write three more questions for a partner.**

Survey
• Do you have a TV in your room?

9 Learner autonomy

Students are encouraged to work independently in a variety of ways, from a carefully guided inductive approach to grammar to self-study worksheets in the Student's Resource Center. This approach makes learning more memorable and supports learner autonomy.

10 Flexible multimedia material

Move Beyond can be used by teachers with limited or no access to technology. But for those wanting to use technology both inside and outside the classroom, the course includes a projectable digital version of the Student's Book as well as a large bank of additional materials and tests in the Online Teacher's Resource Center. Every *Move Beyond* unit contains an original video to supplement the opening lesson.

> We hope you enjoy teaching with *Move Beyond* and that your students enjoy learning with it. We wish you a successful and productive academic year.
>
> *The Move Beyond Team*

Lesson 1 – In the picture

> The first two pages are a single **vocabulary** lesson that serves as an introduction to the unit and its central theme.

Unit themes appeal to teenagers and provide interesting, unusual, and informative material.

1 The lesson starts with a Recall exercise that activates prior knowledge of vocabulary. Recall words are listed in the Words & Beyond section at the back of the book, where students learn and practice a related vocabulary tip.

2 New vocabulary is clearly visible in a word box and is presented and practiced with the support of the images on the pages. Lexical sets are recorded for ease of presentation. Once introduced, vocabulary is recycled throughout the unit and reviewed in the Unit Review and every two units in a Progress Check.

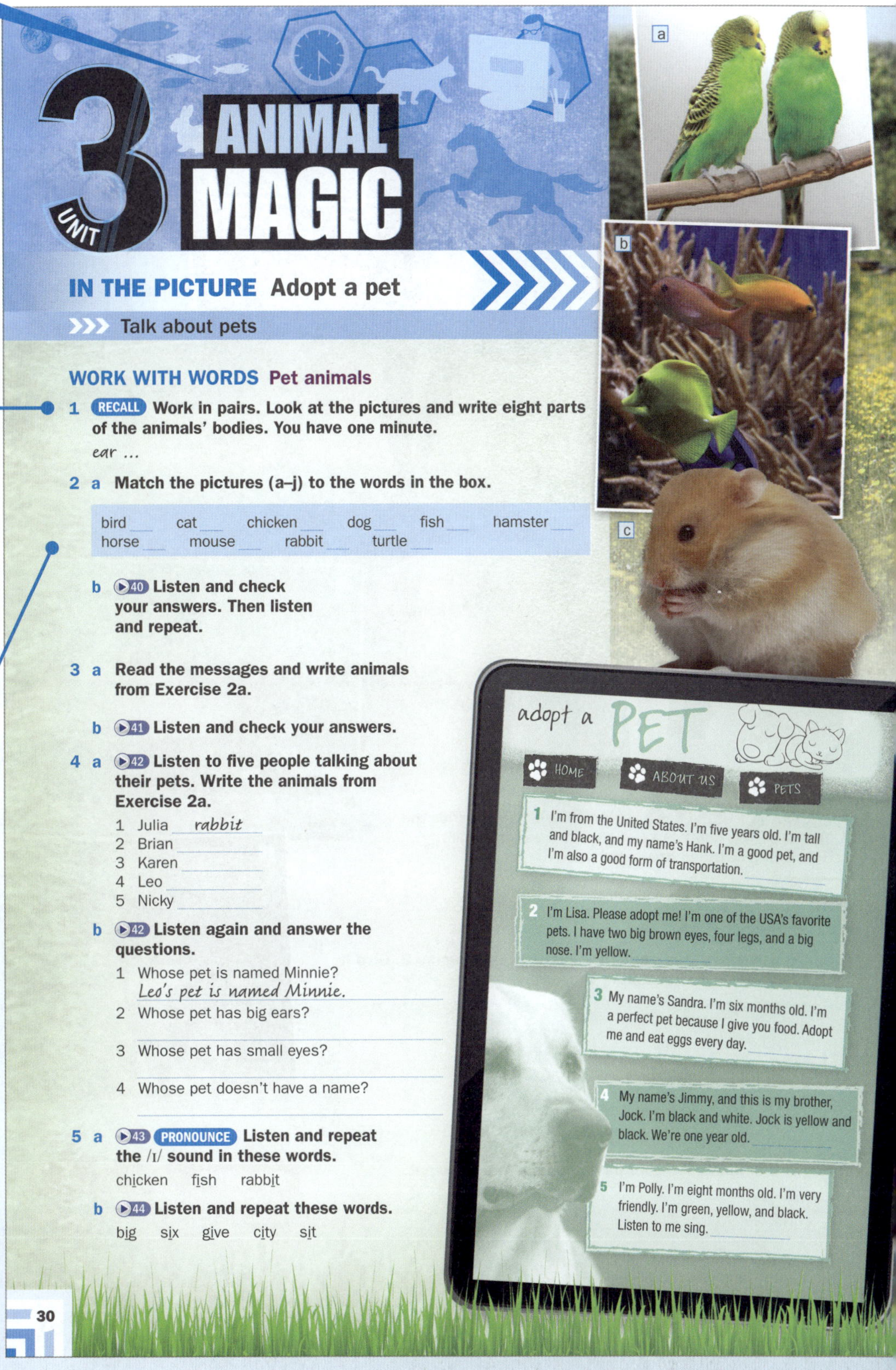

UNIT 3 ANIMAL MAGIC

IN THE PICTURE Adopt a pet

Talk about pets

WORK WITH WORDS Pet animals

1 RECALL **Work in pairs. Look at the pictures and write eight parts of the animals' bodies. You have one minute.**

ear …

2 a **Match the pictures (a–j) to the words in the box.**

bird __ cat __ chicken __ dog __ fish __ hamster __ horse __ mouse __ rabbit __ turtle __

b 40 **Listen and check your answers. Then listen and repeat.**

3 a **Read the messages and write animals from Exercise 2a.**

b 41 **Listen and check your answers.**

4 a 42 **Listen to five people talking about their pets. Write the animals from Exercise 2a.**

1 Julia *rabbit*
2 Brian ____
3 Karen ____
4 Leo ____
5 Nicky ____

b 42 **Listen again and answer the questions.**

1 Whose pet is named Minnie?
Leo's pet is named Minnie.
2 Whose pet has big ears?
3 Whose pet has small eyes?
4 Whose pet doesn't have a name?

5 a 43 PRONOUNCE **Listen and repeat the /ɪ/ sound in these words.**

chicken fish rabbit

b 44 **Listen and repeat these words.**

big six give city sit

a b c

adopt a PET

HOME ABOUT US PETS

1 I'm from the United States. I'm five years old. I'm tall and black, and my name's Hank. I'm a good pet, and I'm also a good form of transportation. ____

2 I'm Lisa. Please adopt me! I'm one of the USA's favorite pets. I have two big brown eyes, four legs, and a big nose. I'm yellow. ____

3 My name's Sandra. I'm six months old. I'm a perfect pet because I give you food. Adopt me and eat eggs every day. ____

4 My name's Jimmy, and this is my brother, Jock. I'm black and white. Jock is yellow and black. We're one year old. ____

5 I'm Polly. I'm eight months old. I'm very friendly. I'm green, yellow, and black. Listen to me sing. ____

30

The unit opener is supported by a video that brings the pages to life. Audio and video are located in the Presentation Kit for ease of access in the classroom and easily available for students on the DVD-ROM.

6 THE MOVING PICTURE ▶ **Watch the video and write the names of the animals you see. Then watch again. How many of the animals are there?**

3 The Moving Picture feature on the opening pages brings a dynamic element to the spread by introducing a video and an accompanying task connected to the lesson.

WRITE AND SPEAK

7 a Choose a pet from one of the pictures in Exercise 2. Give it a new name and complete the form.

TYPE OF ANIMAL: ____
NAME: ____
COLOR: ____
DESCRIPTION: ____

b Work in pairs. Tell your partner about your new pet.

My pet's a/an …
Its name's …
It's …
It has …

MOVE BEYOND

Do the Words & Beyond exercise on page 58.

4 The Move Beyond extras provide material for fast finishers, homework, or additional class activities. The feature refers students to the additional exercises on the Words & Beyond pages at the end of the Student's Book section.

Workbook, page 94

31

5 The final exercises consolidate language with communicative activities in a personalized context.

Lesson 2 – Reading

> After the double-page opening spread, each individual page is one complete lesson. The **reading** and **listening** lessons include an integrated but explicit subskills focus designed to teach students how to read and listen to a variety of text types successfully over the course of a level.

1 The first exercise gives students the opportunity to say what they know or think about the topic of the lesson. This increases confidence and helps students focus on the lesson.

2 Students read a variety of text types and learn the subskills they need to deal successfully with each genre. Reading texts include unusual and original perspectives on familiar topics.

3 The React exercises encourage students to share opinions on the text and relate to it in a personal way.

4 The Move Beyond task provides a further activity related to the content of the reading text.

Subskills are clearly identified.

All texts are recorded to provide extra classroom and self-study opportunities.

Reading texts contain contextualized examples of the grammar point of the next lesson.

There are links to the corresponding Workbook pages (that can be found at the end of the Student's Book) at the bottom of each page.

READING Teach your pet English

>>> Read instructions

SPEAK AND READ

1 Work in pairs. Ask and answer the questions.

1 What pets do you or your friends have?
2 What are their names?

PHRASE BYTES

I have …
My friend has …
Its name's …

READING TIP

Use pictures to help you understand new words.

2 (45) Read the web page. What three things are important to remember?

TEACH YOUR PET ENGLISH!

HOME · ABOUT US · JOKES · CONTACT US

Do you have a pet dog, bird, or rabbit? Do you talk to your pet in Spanish, Turkish, or Russian? Now you can teach your pet English. Use these simple orders and instructions. Don't forget – they aren't for all kinds of pets.

Here are some more unusual instructions …

Remember: Always be nice to your pet. Say …
Good boy! / Good girl!

Finally, here are some more things to say to your pet in English:
Hello / Good morning / Good night (+ name of pet)
Walk time! (It's time for a walk.)
Food! (It's time to eat.)

3 Work in pairs.
Student A: mime an instruction from the web page.
Student B: say the instruction without looking at the page. Then change roles.

PHRASE BYTES

… are popular pets in …
I talk to my … in …
My dad talks to …
Animals understand / don't understand me.

REACT

4 Work in pairs. Ask and answer the questions.

1 Are pets popular in your country? Which ones?
2 Do you talk to animals? In which language?
3 Do animals understand you?

MOVE BEYOND

Write the orders and instructions in the article in your language.

32

Workbook, page 95

Lesson 3 – Grammar (1)

> The target **grammar** is always presented in context, and students are encouraged to figure out rules from examples.

GRAMMAR Imperatives and object pronouns 3

»» Give orders and instructions

READ AND LISTEN »» Grammar in context

1 a Read the conversation. What pet does Laura have – a horse, a chicken, or a hamster?

Mom: Happy birthday, Laura!
Dad: Don't look! OK. Open your eyes.
Laura: Wow, is that for me? A pet ________ !
Mom: It's for you. Find a quiet place for it.
Laura: Is it a boy or a girl?
Mom: It's a boy.
Dad: Don't put him in your room. They play at night.
Mom: Dad has a book for us.
Dad: Yes. It says, "Give them some food and water every day." Don't forget.
Laura: Yes, Dad. Thanks!
Dad: It's all Mom's idea. Thank her!

b 46 Listen and check your answer.

STUDY

2 Complete the examples. Use Exercise 1 to help you.

Imperatives

Affirmative	Negative
Open your eyes.	*Don't look!*
________ *a quiet place for it.*	________ *him in your room.*

See GRAMMAR DATABASE, page 54.

3 Complete the table. Use Exercise 1 to help you.

Object pronouns

Subject pronouns	Object pronouns
It's a boy.	*Find a quiet place for* it.
I	*Is that for* ________ ?
you	*It's for* ________ .
he	*Don't put* ________ *in your room.*
she	*Thank* ________ !
it	*Find a quiet place for* ________ .
we	*Dad has a book for* ________ .
they	*Give* ________ *some food and water every day.*

See GRAMMAR DATABASE, page 54.

»» Workbook, pages 96–97

PRACTICE

4 Choose the correct options to complete the sentences.

TIPS ABOUT HAMSTERS

1 *Keep* / *Don't keep* your hamster in a hot place.
2 *Be* / *Don't be* nice to it.
3 *Give* / *Don't give* it water and food every day.
4 *Say* / *Don't say* bad things to your hamster.
5 *Play* / *Don't play* with it.
6 *Take* / *Don't take* your hamster to your English class.

5 Match the sentences (1–5) to the pictures (a–e).

1 Don't walk on the grass. c
2 Close the door. __
3 Please be quiet. __
4 Don't cross the street. __
5 Don't play ball games. __

6 Complete Laura's teacher's instructions. Use object pronouns.

1 "Class, I'm your teacher and I'm talking. Look at me (your teacher)."
2 "Jack, go to the door and open ________ (the door)."
3 "Helen, find some pens and give ________ (the pens) to Roberto."
4 "Lucas doesn't have his book. Sandra, help ________ (Lucas)."
5 "It's Laura's birthday. Let's say 'Happy birthday' to ________ (Laura)."
6 "Laura, we have something for you. Here's a small present from ________ (me and your classmates)."

SPEAK

7 Work in pairs. Take turns. Give and follow instructions.

Go to the door.
Give me your pen.
Don't talk.

33

1 Target grammar is always presented in context. Students either read or read and listen to a conversation or short text that expands on the theme of the unit.

2 The target grammar is practiced in a controlled but meaningful context that often also provides opportunities for personalization.

3 In the Study section, students are guided to notice grammar structures from the text and then to complete explanations or examples in the Study box.

4 Practice exercises start with more controlled task types and then become progressively freer, preparing students to talk about their own lives and experiences in the Speak or Write and Speak exercise at the end of the lesson.

5 The final tasks focus on speaking and/or writing for accuracy of the target structure within a communicative context.

Lesson 4 – Listening and Vocabulary

> **Listening** comprehension tasks are designed to support understanding and not to test. They progress from a focus on global understanding to an understanding of specific details. The exercises are designed to give practice in a specific listening subskill. Students are always asked to react personally to what they hear.

1 In the Work with Words section, students focus on the second lexical set of the unit. In some units, the Work with Words activity comes before the listening activity in order to introduce new target vocabulary first.

2 As on the reading page, the first exercise ensures that students access their relevant knowledge and experiences before they listen.

3 Listening texts contain contextualized examples of the grammar point of the next lesson, allowing students to hear the language in context before looking at it in depth.

4 The React exercise encourages students to give their personal opinions about the listening text.

5 The Move Beyond task allows students to do a further task related to the new vocabulary set.

LISTENING AND VOCABULARY A new neighbor

››› Listen to a description of a room

WORK WITH WORDS Things in your room

1 Work in pairs. Look at the pictures and answer the questions.

1 What animals can you see in the pictures?
2 Which room is your favorite? Why?

PHRASE BYTES

I can see a / an ...
Room 1 / 2 is my favorite because it has / I like ...

Room 1

Room 2

2 a Match the things in the pictures (a–l) to the words in the box.

bed *e*	chair ___	clock ___	computer ___	desk ___	door ___
floor ___	light ___	picture ___	table ___	wall ___	window ___

b 47 Listen and check. Then listen and repeat.

3 Write the words from Exercise 2a in the correct category.

Parts of a room: *door, ...* **Other things:** *clock, ...*
Furniture: *bed, ...*

SPEAK AND LISTEN

4 48 Listen to the conversation. Which room is it, Room 1 or Room 2?

5 a 48 Answer the questions. Then listen again. Compare your answers with a partner.

1 Who's talking – people or pet animals?
2 Who's the new neighbor – a boy, a girl, a cat, or a dog?
3 What happens at the end?

b Look at page 115 to check your answers.

6 a Complete the sentences with words from Exercise 2.

"Of course there's a (1) *window*. You're looking in it!"
"There's a small (2) ________ next to the bed with a (3) ________ on it."
"There are some (4) ________ on the walls."
"There are two (5) ________. And there's a (6) ________ with a computer."
"Is he there?" – "Yes! He's on the (7) ________."

b 49 Listen and check your answers.

PHRASE BYTES

My favorite room is ...
There's a / an ...

REACT

7 Work in pairs. Ask and answer.

1 What's your favorite room in your house?
2 What things are in that room?

MOVE BEYOND

Do the Words & Beyond exercise on page 58.

34

››› Workbook, pages 98–99

Lesson 5 – Grammar (2)

> The second **grammar** lesson follows the same structure as the first **grammar** lesson of the unit – see page 10.

GRAMMAR *There is / there are* 3

›››Describe a room

READ AND LISTEN ››› Grammar in context

1 (50) **Read and listen to the conversation. What's wrong with the computer room?**

Natalie: What's your English classroom like?
Mario: It's OK. There's a table and a chair for the teacher. There are desks for the students. There are some windows. Oh, and there are some pictures of the USA and the UK on the wall, but there isn't a picture of Australia.
Natalie: Is there a clock?
Mario: Yes, there is. It's next to the door. Why?
Natalie: The questions are for a school survey. Are there any computers?
Mario: No, there aren't. There are computers in the computer room. I don't like the computer room. There aren't any windows.

STUDY

2 a **Complete the table. Use Exercise 1 to help you.**

There is / there are

Use *there is / there are* to describe what's in a place.

Affirmative	Negative
There's a table.	*There **isn't** a picture of Australia.*
There ___*are*___ *(some) desks.*	*There* ______ *any computers.*
Questions	**Short answers**
___*Is*___ *there a clock?*	*Yes, there* ______ *. / No, there isn't.*
___*Are*___ *there any computers?*	*Yes, there are. / No, there* ______ *.*

See GRAMMAR DATABASE, page 54.

b **Underline examples of *there is / there are* in Exercise 1.**

PRACTICE

3 **Look at the picture of Mario's computer room. Are the sentences correct (*C*) or incorrect (*I*)? Rewrite the incorrect sentences.**

1 There are some windows. *I* *There aren't any windows.*
2 There are some brown chairs.
3 There's a clock on the wall.
4 There's one door.
5 There aren't any pictures on the walls.
6 There are three computers.

4 **Write questions about your classroom. Then ask and answer them.**

1 (a clock) *Is there a clock?*
2 (windows) ______
3 (a table for your teacher) ______
4 (pictures on the wall) ______
5 (a bed) ______
6 (computers) ______

5 **Complete the conversation with the correct form of *there is / there are*.**

Natalie: What's your room like?
Mario: OK. (1) ___*There's*___ a bed and a table.
Natalie: (2) ______ a computer on the table?
Mario: No, (3) ______ .
Natalie: (4) ______ any pictures on the walls?
Mario: Yes, there are. (5) ______ some pictures of my favorite soccer team.
Natalie: Is there a window?
Mario: Yes, (6) ______ .

SPEAK

6 **Work in pairs. Complete the tasks.**

- Draw a plan of your room and the things in your room. Don't show it to your partner.
- Ask questions about your partner's room. Make a list of his/her things.
- Compare your list with your partner's plan.

Is there a/an … in your room ?
Are there any … ?
Yes, there is/are.
No, there isn't/aren't.

››› Workbook, page 100

35

1 When applicable, a pronunciation section focuses on misunderstandings that commonly occur when English is used between speakers of different first languages. Pronunciation sections can appear in any lesson, depending on the content, and focus on key sounds and stress patterns in words and sentences.

2 Target vocabulary is recycled throughout the unit.

3 The Grammar Database is a useful reference section where all the grammar points of the level are covered in further detail. You can find additional tips and suggestions for using the Grammar Database in the Teacher's Resource Center.

4 Students are given frequent opportunities to talk about themselves and to express their views.

Lesson 6 – Language & Beyond

> The **Language & Beyond** page is the school skills lesson. The goal of these lessons is to equip students with essential transferable skills needed to help them make a smooth transition from primary school to the increased demands of secondary school. The school skills lessons focus on basic organizational and social skills that can be used in and beyond the classroom.

LANGUAGE & BEYOND

1 A wide range of texts and images is used to raise students' awareness of a particular issue or challenge in their everyday lives.

Prepare your things for school

Working with other students is a key part of the school skills lesson.

SPEAK AND READ

1 a Work in pairs. Look at the pictures for one minute. Then close your books and write the things you remember.

b Open your books and check your lists.

... ebook.
In picture B there are some … .

2 Work in pairs. Which desk is it (A, B, or A and B)?

1 It's before school. *A and B*
2 The desk is neat. ______
3 The homework isn't finished. ______
4 This person's ready for school. ______

2 Students are directed to carry out a practical task in the Do stage. Often working in pairs or small groups, they put themselves in the situation described and think about what they would do.

DO

3 a Do you usually do these things before bed (*A*) or before school (*B*)? Circle your answers.

Do homework	A / B	Ask for bus money	A / B
Prepare clothes for school	A / B	Prepare lunch	A / B
Pack your backpack	A / B	Find keys	A / B

b Where do you usually keep these things – on a table, in your pocket, or in your backpack?

school books keys money pens phone

3 The Reflection Point feature encourages students to pause and think about what they've just done and guides them toward drawing their own conclusions.

4 Work in pairs. Compare your answers to Exercises 3a and 3b. When is the best time to do the things in Exercise 3a? Are the places in Exercise 3b good or bad?

It's good to keep your phone in …
It's bad to keep your money …

REFLECTION POINT

It's good to prepare your school things and do homework before you go to bed. It's good to keep your school things in a special place. You can find them quickly and not be late for school.

REFLECT

5 Talk about the questions. Then read the REFLECTION POINT.

1 When is it good to prepare your school things and do homework?
2 Is it good to keep your school things in one place or different places?
3 Are you ready for school in the morning?

4 The school skills in *Move Beyond* are transferable to classes in other school subjects and to situations outside the classroom. The exercises in the Extend section enable students to apply the skills they have learned in a personalized real-life context.

EXTEND

6 Work in groups. Think of three tips to help students organize their things at school and be ready for each class.

It's good to … / It isn't good to … Keep your things …

PHRASE BYTES

It's good to prepare school things before …
It's good to keep things …
I'm ready / I'm not ready.

Useful phrases help students discuss issues and carry out tasks in English.

SCHOOL SKILLS

36

Workbook, page 103

Lesson 7 – Speaking

> Using real-life scenarios, the **speaking** page provides students with the language they need to communicate effectively in a range of everyday situations. Each speaking lesson helps students develop a specific speaking subskill. Every speaking page features an audio track of teens using the new language in context.

SPEAKING You're welcome 3

>>> Ask for and give things

SPEAK

1 **Work in pairs. What things can you see in the pictures?**

PHRASE BYTES

There's a … There are some …

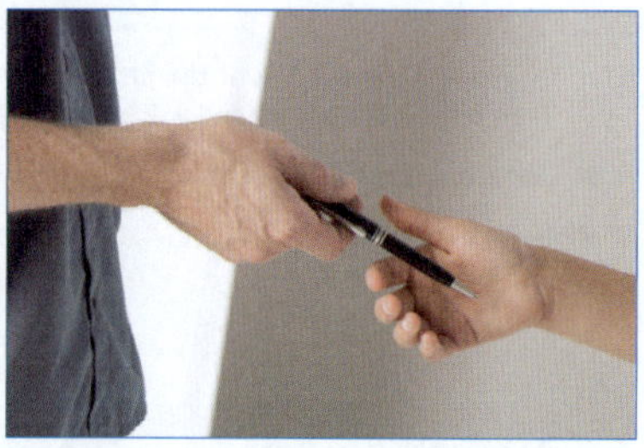

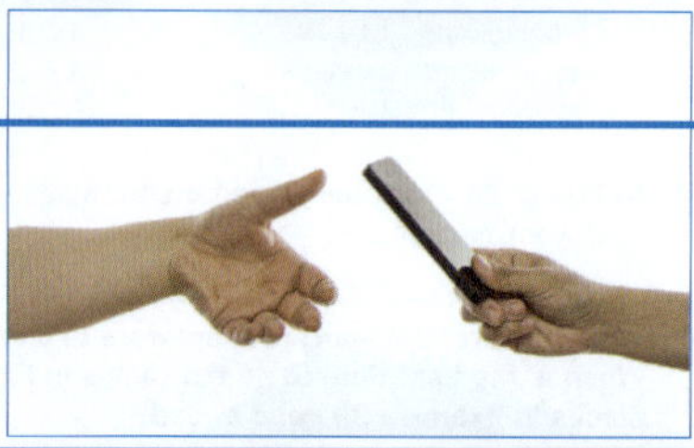

LISTEN

2 a **Complete the conversations and write the missing words. Use the pictures to help you.**

1
Jeff: Can I have some (1) __________ , please?
Lisa: Yes, of course. Here you are.
Jeff: Thanks.
Lisa: You're welcome.

2
Mia: Excuse me. Can I borrow your (2) __________ ?
Brett: Sure. Here you are.
Mia: Thanks.
Brett: You're welcome.

3
Amy: Hi, Kevin. Can I borrow your (3) __________ ?
Kevin: No, sorry.
Amy: Oh. OK.
Donna: You can borrow mine.
Amy: Thanks, Donna.
Donna: You're welcome.

b **51 Listen to the conversations and check your answers.**

3 **Complete the sentences with *have* and *borrow*.**

1 If you ask to __________ something, you don't keep it.
2 If you ask to __________ something, you keep it.

4 **52 Listen and repeat.**

5 **53 Put the sentences in order to make a conversation between Kevin and his dad. Then listen and check.**

__ Please, Dad!
__ OK. Here you are.
__ No, sorry.
__ Thank you.
__ Dad? Can I have some money?
__ You're welcome.

PHRASEBOOK 54

Ask for something
Can I have a / some … , please?
Excuse me. Can I borrow your … ?
Give something
Here you are.
React
Yes, of course.
Sure.
You're welcome.
Thanks.
No, sorry.

ACT

6 **Work in pairs. Complete the tasks.**

- Prepare two conversations – one at school and one at home.
- Use *borrow* in one conversation and *have* in the other.
- Present your conversations to other students.

>>> Workbook, page 101

37

1 The lesson starts with listening or speaking exercises that give students the opportunity to practice functional language.

2 Audio tracks of conversations present students with the context for key functional language. Students listen to conversations and complete an initial gist exercise before focusing on the speaking function or subskill.

3 A variety of exercise types focuses students' attention on the speaking subskill.

4 Each lesson ends with an Act section in which students prepare a conversation of their own to present in groups or to the rest of the class.

5 A **PHRASEBOOK** with relevant functional phrases is provided for use with the Act section of the lesson. This is part of the audio material provided and also serves as a review of speaking subskills.

Lesson 8 – Writing

> The **writing** lesson in each unit allows students to put everything they've learned in the unit into practice. Each writing lesson also develops a specific writing subskill. Students are systematically guided to plan, write, and check their writing in order to produce a final draft.

1 The lesson opens with a short speaking and reading exercise to introduce the topic. Students read a model text and complete a task to check that they have understood the text.

2 The HOW TO feature focuses on a writing subskill and offers tips on how to structure writing and link ideas more effectively.

3 Students do an exercise to practice the subskill they have just learned.

4 Students are given a topic for a writing task and instructed to discuss their ideas first to help them prepare for writing.

5 Students follow a three-step writing plan that guides them to organize their ideas before they begin writing. They are encouraged to refer back to the HOW TO box for support.

6 In the final exercise, students share their work with each other and either write a reply or discuss what they have written.

WRITING Don't forget

»» Write a note

READ

1 Match the notes to the pictures.

a

b

c

1
I'm at Grandma's house. There's some pizza in the kitchen. Be good. Mom.

2
Don't forget! Give Harry some food and water. There's cat food on the table. Sue.

3
William!! Call Barbara before 4 p.m. Basketball practice is at 6 p.m. Dad.

2 Read the notes again and answer the questions.

1 Where's Mom?
2 What's for lunch?
3 Who or what is Harry?
4 Where's Harry's food?
5 Who is Dad's note for?
6 What time is basketball practice?

3 Read the tips in the HOW TO box. Then circle the imperatives in the three notes.

HOW TO
write a note

- Write important information.
- Use imperatives (*Remember* / *Don't forget* ...).
- Don't write long sentences.

PRACTICE

4 Underline the important words in these sentences.

1 Class C: German class is in Room 17 today.
2 Dear Hilary, Enjoy your vacation. Please write and send me a postcard.
3 Don't forget to put the keys on the table for your aunt and uncle.

DISCUSS

5 Talk about work you do at home. Do you help make dinner? Do you feed the dog or cat? Talk about instructions your parents give you to do the job.

WRITE

6 Write a note to give instructions to a family member or friend.

1 Who is the person you are writing to? What instructions does the person need? Is your note about your pet, a school activity, or food?
2 Write your note using imperatives. Remember to start with *Don't* to tell the person not to do something.
3 Write a short note. Don't add information that is not important. Read the tips in the HOW TO box.

SHARE

7 Read your note to other students. Vote on who had the clearest instructions.

38

»» Workbook, pages 102–103

Lesson 9 – Unit Review

> The **Unit Review** page allows students to check and assess their own progress in vocabulary and grammar.

UNIT REVIEW 3

VOCABULARY Pet animals

1 Write the words for the pets.

WELCOME TO THE *Pet Hotel*. ALL PETS ARE WELCOME!

1 d ___
2 r ___
3 c ___
4 m ___
5 b ___
6 t ___
7 h ___
8 c ___
9 f ___
10 h ___

Things in your room

2 Choose the correct options to complete the text.

Pet Hotel HOME ABOUT RESERVATIONS

All our rooms have four (1) *clocks* / *walls* , a (2) *door* / *floor* (with a special key), a big (3) *bed* / *window* to look at the street, and a (4) *floor* / *picture* (if you don't sleep in a bed).

There's a big (5) *bed* / *table* to sleep on (if you don't like the floor). There's a small (6) *light* / *table* next to the bed with a (7) *light* / *table* on it. If you want the internet, sit on the (8) *chair* / *computer* at the (9) *desk* / *door* and use the (10) *computer* / *window* . It's free!

What time is it? Look at the (11) *clock* / *picture* on the wall. There's also a (12) *table* / *picture* of me on the wall. Have a nice stay!

___ /12

GRAMMAR Imperatives and object pronouns

3 Complete the text with the words and phrases in the box.

come don't forget don't stay eat him them us you

Pet Hotel HOME ABOUT RESERVATIONS

Are you an animal? (1) ________ in a normal hotel. (2) ________ to the Pet Hotel! At the Pet Hotel, we really understand (3) ________ . (4) ________ in the Pet Hotel's famous restaurant. Talk to our chef, Mr. Rex, and tell (5) ________ your favorite food. Make new animal friends and relax with (6) ________ in our yard. (7) ________ the name – the Pet Hotel. Call (8) ________ now at 1-800-PET-HOTEL!

___ /16

There is / there are

4 Match the sentence halves.

Pet Hotel HOME ABOUT RESERVATIONS

Any questions?

1 Is there ___
2 Yes, ___
3 There's a ___
4 Are there any ___
5 No. There aren't any ___
6 There are some ___

a big yard with a lot of grass.
b people at the hotel.
c there is.
d a yard?
e birds, dogs, cats, and one elephant.
f people at the Pet Hotel?

___ / 12

Your score: ___ / 50

SKILLS CHECK

✓✓✓ Yes, I can. No problem!
✓✓ Yes, I can. But I need a little help.
✓ Yes, I can. But I need a lot of help.

I can read instructions. ___
I can listen to a description of a room. ___
I can prepare my things for school. ___
I can ask for and give things. ___
I can write a note. ___

Workbook, pages 104–105

39

The exercises in the Unit Review are all set in a single context and reflect the way language is used in real life.

Each exercise has a space for students to record their scores.

1 The Unit Review starts with two exercises to test the two lexical sets covered in the unit.

2 Two grammar exercises test the two grammar points covered in the unit.

3 After completing the exercises, students calculate their total score. Each review has the same overall score so that students can assess their progress across units.

4 Students are encouraged to self-assess their progress using CEFR "can-do" statements that refer directly back to the objectives of the skills pages.

Progress Check

> After every two units, there is a two-page skills-based **Progress Check** that allows students and teachers to see how well the learning objectives in the preceding two units have been met. Tasks on these pages reflect those that students will see on standardized English exams. The Progress Checks also include tips on how to deal successfully with the various tasks.

1 Progress Check tasks consolidate the language from the preceding two units.

2 The Test-Taking Tips help students prepare for standard exam-style tasks.

PROGRESS CHECK

READ

1 Read the sentences about Oliver's free time. Choose the best word (A, B, or C) for each blank.

TEST-TAKING TIPS

complete sentences with multiple-choice answers

- Look at the example.
- Read each sentence and the choices (A, B, or C).
- Decide which words are wrong. For each word, check:
  - Does it have the correct meaning?
  - Can you use it with the words before and after it?
- Read the sentence again. Check your answer.

Example:

0 In the evening I ___ television.
A look B see (C) watch

1 After school I go on the ___ .
A internet B movies C shopping

2 I listen ___ music on my phone.
A at B with C to

3 My favorite kind ___ music is Latin.
A in B of C at

4 I can play the ___ .
A soccer B piano C video games

5 I ___ my friends on weekends.
A play B listen C meet

Reading: _______ /10

50

PROGRESS CHECK 3&4

LISTEN

2 70 **Listen to Delia and Luke. What animals or pets do the people in Delia's family have? For questions 1–5, write the correct letter (A–H) next to each person.**

Example:
0 Mom B

PEOPLE		PETS	
1 Dad		A bird	E mouse
2 her brother		B cat	F fish
3 her sister		C chickens	G horse
4 Grandma		D dog	H hamster
5 Grandpa			

Listening: ______ /10

TEST-TAKING TIPS

match things in two lists

- Read both lists.
- Listen for the words in the lists.
- Use only five of the words from A–H.

WRITE

3 Complete Alice's email to her friend. For questions 1–10, write one word for each blank.

Example:
0 ___for___

New mail ← Reply → Forward

Dear Lucia,
Thanks (0) ___for___ your email about your free time. On school days I (1) ________ homework after school. On weekends I (2) ________ my bike or I (3) ________ shopping with my mom. I have (4) ________ dog. Her name's Cookie. I take (5) ________ to the park at a quarter (6) ________ seven every morning. She's old and a little deaf, so she (7) ________ hear me. But she's a smart dog. She (8) ________ play soccer! Do you (9) ________ a pet?
(10) ________ soon!
Alice

Writing: ______ / 10

Progress check score ______ /30

TEST-TAKING TIPS

complete a text with blanks

- First, read the text quickly.
- Look at the words before and after each blank.
- Use only one word in the blank.
- Use the correct form of verbs. Check your spelling.

51

Other features

At the end of the Student's Book material, you'll find the following resources:

Grammar Database
The Grammar Database provides detailed additional explanations of the grammar points of each unit, as well as grammar tables and common errors to watch out for. It is a valuable reference section for students.

Words & Beyond
These pages contain lists of the main lexical sets from each unit, as well as other important vocabulary from the unit, vocabulary tips, and additional tasks.

Irregular verbs
A list of common irregular verbs is provided for students' reference.

Extras
The material for pairwork activities (with Student A and Student B) from the units is provided here, as well as answers to quiz questions.

3 Overall scoring is the same in every Progress Check, so students can monitor both their overall progress and their progress in specific skills.

USING THE *MOVE BEYOND* WORKBOOK

The *Move Beyond* Workbook lessons recontextualize, review, and recycle target items from the corresponding lesson pages of the Student's Book and offer comprehensive practice for homework and class use.

- Two vocabulary pages per unit practice the target vocabulary in new contexts.
- Intuitive instructions make it easier to complete each exercise.
- Puzzles and games add an element of fun and variety.

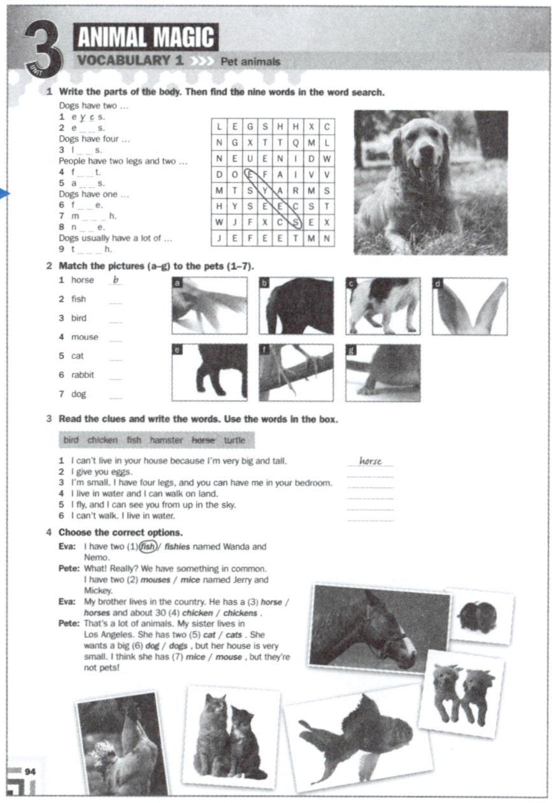

3 ANIMAL MAGIC
VOCABULARY 1 ››› Pet animals

1 Write the parts of the body. Then find the nine words in the word search.

Dogs have two ...
1 e y e s.
2 e _ _ s.
Dogs have four ...
3 l _ _ s.
People have two legs and two ...
4 f _ _ t.
5 a _ _ s.
Dogs have one ...
6 f _ _ e.
7 m _ _ h.
8 n _ _ e.
Dogs usually have a lot of ...
9 t _ _ _ h.

L	E	G	S	H	H	X	C
N	G	X	T	T	Q	M	L
N	E	U	E	N	I	D	W
D	O	E	F	A	I	V	V
M	T	S	Y	A	R	M	S
H	Y	S	E	E	C	S	T
W	J	F	X	C	S	E	X
J	E	F	E	E	T	M	N

2 Match the pictures (a–g) to the pets (1–7).
1 horse b
2 fish
3 bird
4 mouse
5 cat
6 rabbit
7 dog

3 Read the clues and write the words. Use the words in the box.

bird chicken fish hamster ~~horse~~ turtle

1 I can't live in your house because I'm very big and tall. horse
2 I give you eggs.
3 I'm small. I have four legs, and you can have me in your bedroom.
4 I live in water and I can walk on land.
5 I fly, and I can see you from up in the sky.
6 I can't walk. I live in water.

4 Choose the correct options.
Eva: I have two (1) (fish) / fishies named Wanda and Nemo.
Pete: What! Really? We have something in common. I have two (2) mouses / mice named Jerry and Mickey.
Eva: My brother lives in the country. He has a (3) horse / horses and about 30 (4) chicken / chickens.
Pete: That's a lot of animals. My sister lives in Los Angeles. She has two (5) cat / cats. She wants a big (6) dog / dogs, but her house is very small. I think she has (7) mice / mouse, but they're not pets!

94

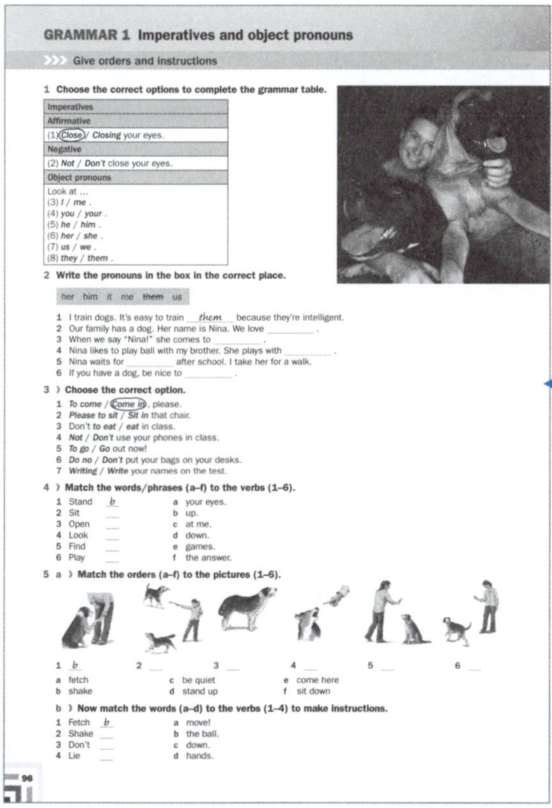

GRAMMAR 1 Imperatives and object pronouns
››› Give orders and instructions

1 Choose the correct options to complete the grammar table.

Imperatives
Affirmative
(1) (Close) / Closing your eyes.
Negative
(2) Not / Don't close your eyes.
Object pronouns
Look at ... (3) I / me. (4) you / your. (5) he / him. (6) her / she. (7) us / we. (8) they / them.

2 Write the pronouns in the box in the correct place.

her him it me ~~them~~ us

1 I train dogs. It's easy to train them because they're intelligent.
2 Our family has a dog. Her name is Nina. We love ______.
3 When we say "Nina!" she comes to ______.
4 Nina likes to play ball with my brother. She plays with ______.
5 Nina waits for ______ after school. I take her for a walk.
6 If you have a dog, be nice to ______.

3 › Choose the correct option.
1 To come / (Come in), please.
2 Please to sit / Sit in that chair.
3 Don't to eat / eat in class.
4 Not / Don't use your phones in class.
5 To go / Go out now!
6 Do no / Don't put your bags on your desks.
7 Writing / Write your names on the test.

4 › Match the words/phrases (a–f) to the verbs (1–6).
1 Stand b — a your eyes.
2 Sit — b up.
3 Open — c at me.
4 Look — d down.
5 Find — e games.
6 Play — f the answer.

5 a › Match the orders (a–f) to the pictures (1–6).
1 b 2 __ 3 __ 4 __ 5 __ 6 __
a fetch b shake c be quiet d stand up e come here f sit down

b › Now match the words (a–d) to the verbs (1–4) to make instructions.
1 Fetch b — a move!
2 Shake — b the ball.
3 Don't — c down.
4 Lie — d hands.

96

- The Workbook contains three pages per unit for practicing target grammar.
- Grammar Study boxes review the form and use of key grammar.
- Students then practice through contextualized grammar exercises.
- Exercises on the Grammar pages are presented in order of difficulty, shown by chevrons (› = easiest, ›› = medium challenge, ››› = most difficult).

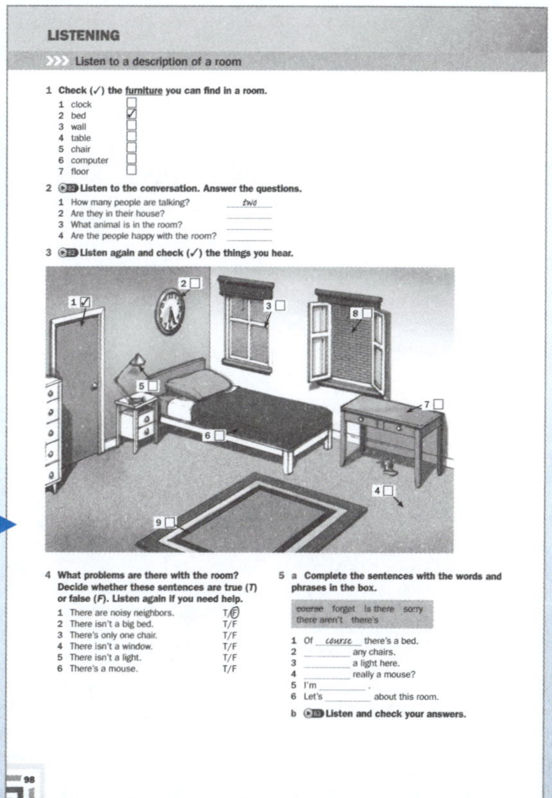

LISTENING
››› Listen to a description of a room

1 Check (✓) the furniture you can find in a room.
1 clock
2 bed ✓
3 wall
4 table
5 chair
6 computer
7 floor

2 Listen to the conversation. Answer the questions.
1 How many people are talking? two
2 Are they in their house?
3 What animal is in the room?
4 Are the people happy with the room?

3 Listen again and check (✓) the things you hear.

4 What problems are there with the room? Decide whether these sentences are true (T) or false (F). Listen again if you need help.
1 There are noisy neighbors. T/F
2 There isn't a big bed. T/F
3 There's only one chair. T/F
4 There isn't a window. T/F
5 There isn't a light. T/F
6 There's a mouse. T/F

5 a Complete the sentences with the words and phrases in the box.

~~course~~ forget Is there sorry there aren't there's

1 Of course there's a bed.
2 ______ any chairs.
3 ______ a light here.
4 ______ really a mouse?
5 I'm ______.
6 Let's ______ about this room.

b Listen and check your answers.

98

- Key listening subskills from the Student's Book are reintroduced and reexamined.
- Exercises put these skills into practice and review target language.
- Additional listening exercises focus on the theme of the unit, often through test-style tasks related to the subskill in the lesson.

USING THE *MOVE BEYOND* WORKBOOK

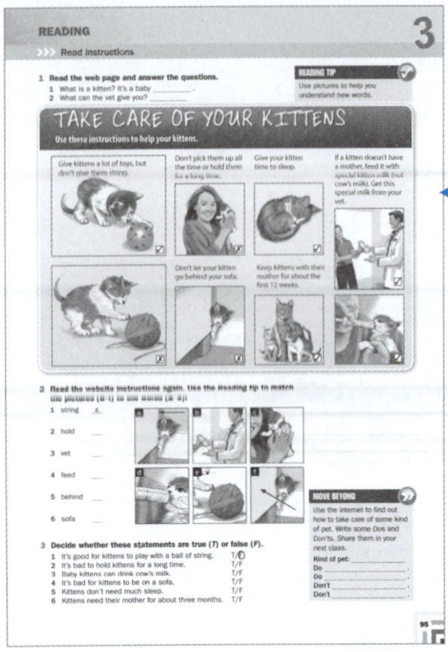

- Texts build on the themes introduced in the Student's Book.
- Tasks focus on putting reading subskills into practice, recycling key language, and exposing students to test-style tasks.

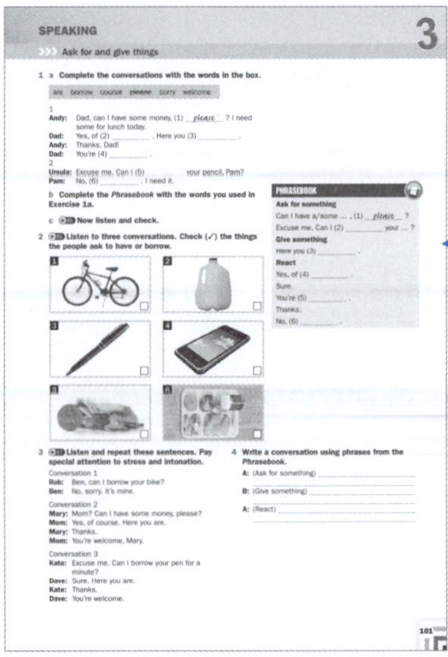

- The speaking lesson focuses on reviewing key lexical items.
- Target items are presented in context, and recordings are frequently used to focus on important aspects of speaking, such as register, stress, and intonation.

- REMEMBER HOW TO boxes focus on key subskills from the Student's Book lessons.
- Key writing subskills from the Student's Book are developed in exercises carefully designed to practice the skill.
- Emphasis is put on the planning and structuring of texts, and students are guided through final exam-type writing tasks.

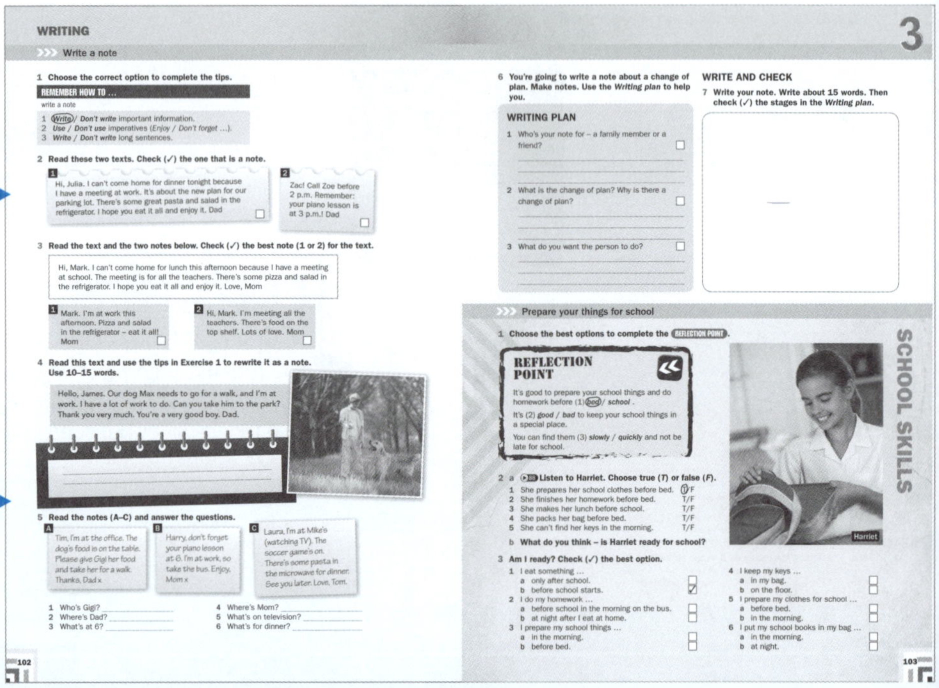

- The school skill of the unit is revisited, and students are challenged to apply the skill in a personalized new context.

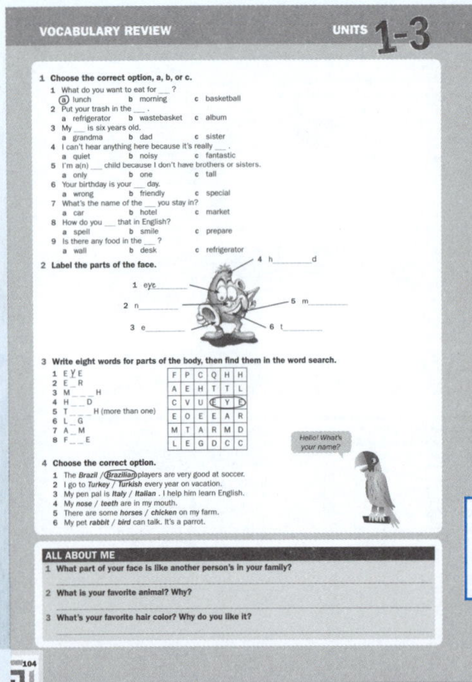

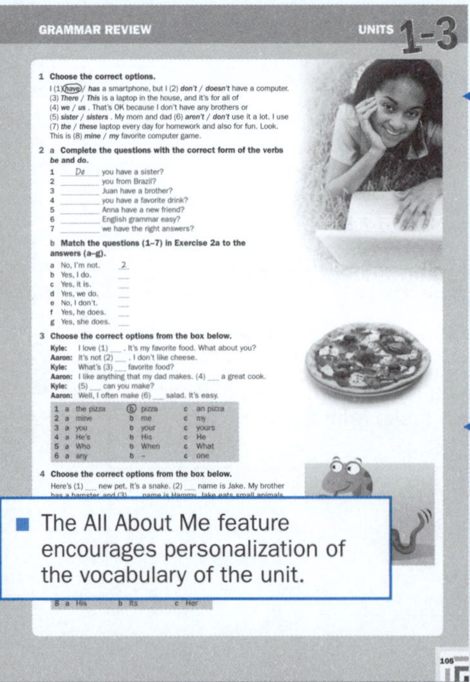

- Target vocabulary and grammar taken from any units of the Student's Book covered to date are recontextualized and reviewed here, allowing students to monitor their own progress.

- The review pages offer cumulative assessment, with exercises combining two or more grammar points or vocabulary sets.

- The All About Me feature encourages personalization of the vocabulary of the unit.

MOVE BEYOND DIGITAL

The digital components of ***Move Beyond*** are easy to integrate into your regular classroom activities. The range of multimedia resources gives teachers an excellent opportunity to digitize their lessons and present the material in different ways, which varies the pace and dynamics in the classroom. Classwork, homework, and testing are all accommodated in the ***Move Beyond*** Teacher's Resource Center, where plenty of flexible additional materials for both online and offline use can be found.

Go to mee2.macmillaneducation.com to access:

- *Move Beyond Intro A Level* Presentation Kit, consisting of a digital Student's Book designed for classroom presentation
- *Move Beyond Intro A Level* Teacher's Resource Center, for extra materials, tests, videos, and downloadable audio.

Teacher's Resource Center

The Teacher's Resource Center provides teachers with downloadable extra grammar and vocabulary worksheets, tips, and testing materials to support the course. It contains a whole range of additional ***Move Beyond*** materials to be used in the classroom or assigned for homework, as well as access to everything in the Student's Resource Center.

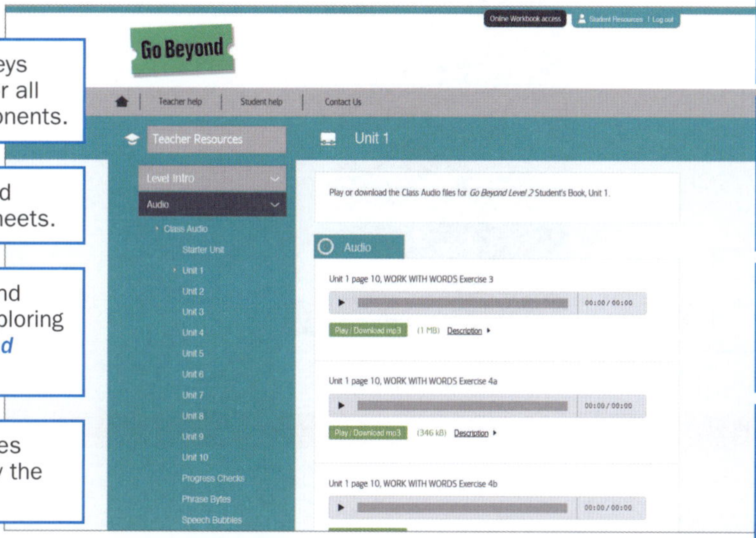

Full answer keys and scripts for all course components.

Extra Grammar and Vocabulary worksheets.

Further ideas and activities for exploring the ***Move Beyond*** videos.

Teacher's notes to accompany the worksheets.

Tips and model answers to accompany the Student's Book and Workbook writing tasks.

A teacher-delivered speaking section to accompany every Student's Book Progress Check.

Static PDF tests for each unit and for the beginning, middle, and end of each level.

A link to special ***Move Beyond*** materials on www.onestopenglish.com, as well as access to other useful onestopenglish resources.

MOVE BEYOND DIGITAL

Presentation Kit

The Presentation Kit includes a projectable digital version of the ***Move Beyond*** Student's Book for teachers to use in class to promote "eyes-up" learning and student interaction. Easily downloadable to multiple devices from mee2.macmillaneducation.com, the Presentation Kit can also be used for lesson preparation at home.

Once downloaded, the Presentation Kit can be used offline. Audio recordings, videos, and answer keys are embedded in the pages for easy reference along with optional pop-up audio scripts and video subtitles, which are synched to the content. There are also fully interactive exercises to work through as a class.

Move easily between the pages of the Student's Book.

Play the video in situ.

Show the answer key instantly, alongside the exercise.

Do an interactive version of the exercise in class and get instant feedback.

Play the class audio in situ.

Annotate the pages using built-in tools.

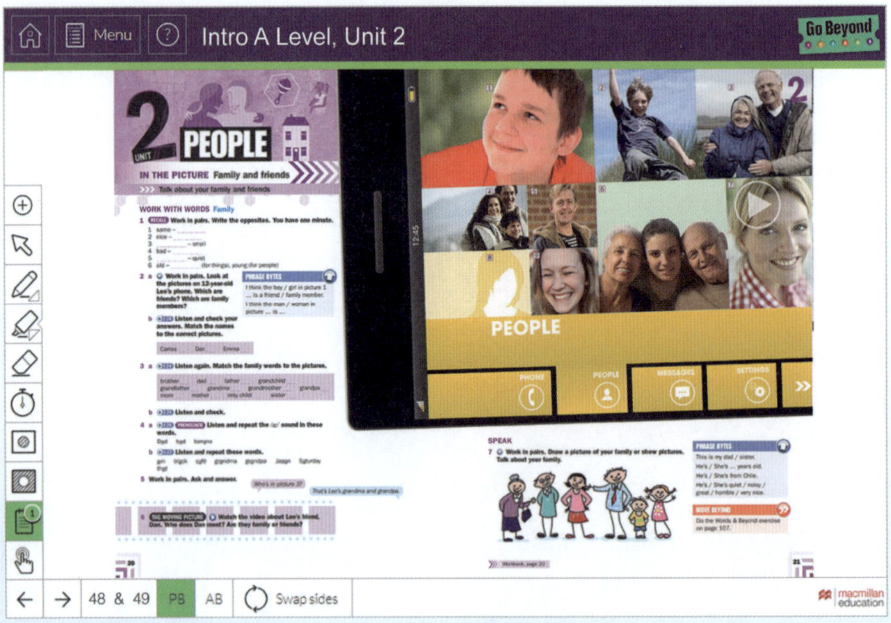

Move Beyond videos

There is a video for each *Move Beyond* unit, adding richness and variety to the material. The Moving Picture videos from the opening spreads bring global experiences into the classroom. The videos include documentary clips, vox pops, slideshows, digital animation, and YouTube-style videos. These engaging visuals support listening skills and act as conversation starters.

The *Move Beyond* videos are embedded in the Presentation Kit and supplied on a DVD-ROM at the back of the combined Student's Book/Workbook. Teachers can also access them at home via the Teacher's Resource Center.

From The Moving Picture video, Unit 7.

Video tips

You can extend the activities or use the videos separately by using some of these video tips.

From the Moving Picture Video, Unit 2.

Before you watch

Students can predict what they'll see and hear in the video.

- Show students the title of the video or give them the topic and ask them to brainstorm vocabulary they think will come up.
- Show the video using the "Fast forward" option or show one or two stills from the video and ask students to predict what is happening or what people are saying.
- Show the first few seconds of the video and ask students to predict what will happen next.

While you watch

You can ask students to watch the videos normally or use just the picture or audio.

A Picture with no sound

- In pairs, one student watches and describes what he or she sees to a partner, who takes notes. They then watch together and discuss differences.
- Make a worksheet with screen shots from scenes in the video. Students write their own dialog or complete speech bubbles.
- Students write their own script for what they see. They then speak over the video, providing the narration or character voices. Finally, they compare their version to the original.

B Sound with no picture

- Students listen to the sound only and speculate in pairs/groups about what they hear. They then watch to see if they were right.

C Picture and sound

- Students make notes as they watch and then compare notes with a partner or in groups.
- After showing the video the first time, give students cards with key words or phrases from the video. As students watch the video a second time, ask them to hold up their cards each time they hear a key word or phrase from their cards in the video.

After you watch

Use these activities in conjunction with the Before/While you watch activities or as your main activity.

- Students create a fictional story, write a news story, or do a role-play based on the video or part of it.
- Students write an email or a text message to somebody in the video. They can also make a brochure, ad, fact file, or poster related to a topic or place in the video.
- Show students still photos of people from the video and ask them to make a brief biography for that person – name, age, nationality, family, likes and dislikes, hobbies, and favorite food.

TEACHING TIPS

To optimize your teaching experience with ***Move Beyond***, we've put together some tips for the following key areas:

- Classroom management
- Teaching vocabulary and grammar
- Teaching skills
- Teaching pronunciation

Classroom management

Managing a classroom of teenagers is not always easy, and good classroom management, including organizing resources, creating an effective learning environment, monitoring student progress, and anticipating potential obstacles to learning, is crucial for keeping students on track. The following tips will help you maximize the time in the classroom and ensure a productive learning environment.

Setting up routines and procedures

Let students familiarize themselves with classroom procedures and homework routines early on in the year. This helps create a well-managed, organized classroom, especially with large classes.

Students in large classes may find it difficult to hear instructions, so pay special attention to giving instructions clearly. *Everyone open your books. Stand up, everyone!* etc. Set up a signal to get students' attention (e.g., clapping your hands or whistling). One strategy that works well is to raise an arm and put your finger on your lips for students to notice the signal and respond.

If routines and procedures are established at the beginning of the year, the rest of the year will be more enjoyable and productive for both you and your students.

Pairwork

Pairwork is essential for speaking practice. In large classes it may not be practical for students to trade seats freely. However, you can simply ask students to turn to the person sitting next to them for pairwork or to turn around to form pairs or fours with those seated behind. You can change pairings by instructing the students seated at the end of each row of chairs to move to the front of their respective rows – and then get everyone else to move along one seat.

Open and closed pairs

An open pair is when a pair of students work together with the rest of the class observing. It can help less confident students understand the instructions and highlight the language they will need for an activity. Be sensitive and choose more confident students to demonstrate the activity. Avoid individual error correction at this stage.

Closed pairs means that students are working in pairs all at the same time. Closed pairwork is important because it gives students a chance to explore new language privately; it is also useful for teachers because you can walk around and monitor students and give individual feedback.

Giving students time to think

Students sometimes take longer to reply than you might expect. It's a good idea to wait about three seconds for students to first process a question and then formulate a response. This waiting time will encourage students and should give them more confidence in their responses.

Checking answers 1

Keep students alert and motivated by varying the ways you select them to answer questions. Alternate between calling on students to give answers and asking for volunteers. This will help keep them engaged and get all the students involved in the process of checking answers.

You could also call on a student and let him or her decide which question to answer. This is good for less confident students. It is then fun to let that student choose who will answer the next question.

Alternatively, if you have closely monitored students while they were doing the activity, "randomly" call on the students who have the correct answers. Both of these techniques are good for giving students confidence in speaking and sharing their answers in class.

Checking answers 2

Students appreciate the opportunity to look at a partner's answers for reassurance. This technique helps create a productive learning environment. If students compare their answers, they'll have more confidence in them and therefore will be much more likely to volunteer them. This also gives students an opportunity to use English to explain why they chose their answer and helps develop their ability to compare and discuss in English.

Point out to students, whenever possible, that making mistakes is positive. Remind students that the most successful learners are usually the ones who aren't afraid to experiment and make mistakes.

Correcting errors effectively

It is important not to overcorrect, as this can make students lose confidence. However, undercorrecting leads to students developing bad language habits and decreases their communicative abilities in the long run.

When students are carrying out pairwork activities, the focus is on fluency and it is best not to correct errors. However, monitor students and note important errors and good use of language to go over at the end of the activity in a feedback session. Dedicate a few minutes of class time to error correction. Write the errors on the board without saying who made the mistakes and elicit correct answers from the class.

Total Physical Response

Total Physical Response (TPR) is a teaching method where instructors give instructions and students respond with whole-body movements. TPR activities could be as basic as following instructions to *sit down, stand up,* or *pick up your pen,* and TPR lends itself well to games such as *Simon Says*.

TPR can be motivating and fun for students and is especially popular with learners who don't like to be sitting down for too long and with kinesthetic learners. Although it may seem unrealistic to sustain a whole lesson by giving commands and repeating them, activities like this can break up the class and reduce stress, as students are not under pressure to produce the target language and simply have to respond to it.

Teaching vocabulary and grammar

Intro Contracted forms

A contraction is two words joined together to make a short form. The verb *be* is often shortened. We use an apostrophe (') in place of the missing letters. Contractions are common in spoken English and informal writing. We don't usually use contractions in formal writing. We can make contractions only with certain words. There are three common types.

- Subject + affirmative auxiliary (e.g., *I'd*, *I've*)
- Negative sentences with *not* (e.g., *don't*, *isn't*)
- Question words + *is* (e.g., *When's*, *Where's*)

Intro English plural nouns

In order to change a singular noun to its plural form in English, you usually add *-s* (e.g., *bags, days*). These are regular plurals. However, there are many irregular plurals that do not follow this rule:

- Nouns that end in *ch, x, s, z,* or *sh* sounds require an *-es* for the plural (e.g., *boxes, sandwiches, buses*).
- Several nouns have irregular forms (e.g., *women, children, men, people*).
- Nouns that end in a consonant + *-y* drop the *-y* and add *-ies* (e.g., *cities*, *parties*).
- Many nouns that end in *-o* take *-es* in the plural (e.g., *tomat**oes**, potat**oes***).

Intro Possessive adjectives and possessive pronouns

Students often confuse possessive adjectives and possessive pronouns. Possessive adjectives are placed directly before the noun they modify to show possession; for example:

My bag is heavy.
His coat is blue.
Our sneakers are on the floor.

Possessive pronouns are used to say who an item or an idea belongs to. Possessive pronouns are used only when the object of possession (the thing that is *yours, hers, ours,* etc.) is understood from the context. In other words, they replace a noun that has previously been referred to. The possessive pronoun is then used to clarify to whom the object belongs; for example:

The heavy bag is mine.
The blue coat is his. Mine is white.
The sneakers on the floor are ours.

Point out that possessive pronouns are not spelled with an apostrophe.

Word lists

When students learn new words, it is important to encourage them to keep a record of them in a separate book or at the back of their notebooks. As they do this, encourage them to group the words into categories as this will help them make further associations, and they will be more likely to remember the words. Possible categories for making word lists are:

Positives and negatives: *happy/unhappy*
Opposites: *cold/hot*
Topic/theme: *Family – mother, father, aunt, uncle*

Remembering new words

Recommend to students that they spend up to 10 minutes every day writing lists of vocabulary in English and saying these words aloud. The more they repeat this procedure, the more they will familiarize themselves with the words. Students can surround themselves with English by labeling their homes with stickers or sticky notes. Ask students to think of their own method for remembering vocabulary and to try it for a month. At the end of the month, ask them to give feedback to the class on whether their method was successful.

Intro Countable and uncountable nouns

Countable nouns (e.g., *potato, vegetable, chip,* etc.) have singular and plural forms and can be counted easily. The singular form can take the article *a/an*, and regular plural forms end in *-s/-es*. There are also irregular forms such as *man/men*, *child/children*, and *person/people*.

Uncountable nouns (e.g., *pasta, spaghetti, salad,* etc.) have only one form and cannot be counted easily. They are sometimes referred to as mass nouns.

There are several potential problems for learners.

- It is not always obvious that the noun is countable, especially with some irregular plurals such as *children*, so students may add an *-s*.
- An uncountable word may be countable in L1. For example, when talking about *news* (uncountable) students may try to use the incorrect singular form, ~~*a new*~~ (rather than *a piece/an item of news*).
- In some cases, students may not use articles for singular nouns, especially if they wouldn't in L1. For example, in some languages, jobs are not preceded by an article: ~~*My father is lawyer*~~.
- Some nouns can be both countable and uncountable; for example: *I try to eat fruit every day.* (uncountable) / *There are some fruits that I don't like, for example, grapefruit.* (countable)

You can review countable and uncountable nouns throughout the course. When students have finished reading a text or audio script, have them find as many examples as they can of each type of noun in the text.

Teaching skills

Writing

Correcting written work

If writing is assigned for homework, or if you collect your students' work at the end of a writing activity, you can correct it for students to copy their mistakes or rewrite the text. When grading students' written work, it is important to think about the level of your students and decide which mistakes they can correct themselves.

Remember to add a comment at the end to show interest and to praise the student if possible. Using a correction sheet, with symbols and acronyms, to mark students' work can save you time. Give students a copy of the correction sheet to guide them toward correcting their own mistakes. You can also list mistakes that are common to students and provide some interesting expressions and good use of language in a general feedback session on the writing homework at the beginning of the next class.

Punctuation

Punctuation helps the reader understand when to pause between fully formed ideas when speaking, and it helps us organize our thoughts when writing.

A classic way to point out to students how important punctuation can be is to put this sentence on the board and ask them to punctuate it.

Let's eat Grandpa

Check to see who has written the first or the second line.

Let's eat Grandpa.

Let's eat, Grandpa.

Correct punctuation can save lives!

Giving feedback on written work done in class

Having students do writing tasks in class provides a good opportunity to focus on individual students. Circulate around the class and make sure that students are on task. Give positive feedback and help them with any problems they may have. While you're doing this, note good language and common errors to put on the board at the end of the activity. Then ask students to identify sentences that are correct and to correct the errors in the other sentences. You could make this a team activity and award points for correct answers.

Making it a group activity

Try to incorporate group work into writing lessons so that it is not always a solitary activity. Put students into small groups to work on the processes of writing: brainstorming, planning, structuring, drafting, and reviewing.

Speaking

Being polite

Being polite depends as much on intonation as on use of language, and students should be encouraged to be aware of their attitude when they make polite requests (smiling, correct intonation, etc.).

Point out to students that we use either *Excuse me* at the beginning or *please* at the end, but we don't usually use both in the same request.

Disappearing conversation

In this activity, students are given support to help them recall a conversation from memory. Start by writing a short conversation on the board and having students practice it in pairs. Then erase some of the words and have students practice again. You can keep removing words until students are left with just prompt words or no words at all.

This activity gives students the chance to practice paraphrasing and using synonyms, as well as testing their memories.

Class discussions

When inviting students to share answers and opinions with the class, it is a good idea to make sure that the interaction is among students in the class, and not only between the students and the teacher. Rather than giving your opinion, ask other students if they agree, and ask them to give their reasons. Develop the conversation by inviting other students to share their opinions. At this level students may require clear guidelines, so you could put some useful expressions on the board (*What do you think? I think, I'm not sure, It depends*, etc.) and encourage students to use them.

Checking that you understand

Students often find it embarrassing when they don't understand what someone has said in English and are unsure how to ask for clarification. It is important to reassure students that even native speakers have to ask for clarification sometimes. Give them some useful phrases to do this:

Showing you don't understand	Asking for clarification
I don't understand. *I'm not sure I understand.* *Sorry, I didn't quite hear what you said.* *Sorry, I didn't get your point.*	*What do you mean by … ?* *Do you mean … ?* *Could you say that again, please?* *Could you repeat that, please?*

Listening

Recorded reading texts

The reading texts are recorded so that students can listen to them as they read or with books closed. The recorded material gives students extra exposure to correct pronunciation: word and sentence stress, intonation, and accent. It also brings the text to life and adds interest. Suggestions for how to use the recorded reading texts are included at the end of each reading lesson.

Listening for the main idea

Many students experience anxiety and need help learning to listen effectively. Often students try to listen for everything, and they're not in control of the process that leads to comprehension. One important skill is to learn to identify the gist – the main ideas – of a conversation, before breaking down the information and concentrating on the details they need to complete a task. Encourage students to relax and not to worry if they don't understand every word on the first listening. Ask them to focus on picking out words that seem to be "highlighted" with special stress and/or repetition, as these will probably signal the topic and main ideas of a conversation.

Listening for specific information

Students often want to try to understand everything. A key strategy to help students focus on listening for specific information is to encourage them to prepare for the task by looking closely at the questions. They can use the questions to get an idea of the context of the listening and to predict what kind of information they need to listen for in order to complete the task. The words in the task help guide them through the listening and help them identify where they should concentrate their efforts and listen intensively.

Encouraging prediction

Predicting content is something that we all do in our first language before and while we are listening.

- **Predict the topic.** Where possible, draw students' attention to any images on the Student's Book page and ask them what they think the topic will be.
- **Predict the speakers.** Hand out printouts of the audio script for a chosen conversation in the Student's Book. Ask students to cover the speakers' names with a piece of paper, and then ask them to read the conversation and guess the age, gender, and relationship between the speakers. Write their ideas on the board, and after you have listened to the audio, check whether any of their guesses were correct.
- **Predict the word.** While playing the audio track, press the pause button mid-sentence and ask students if they can predict the next word. Repeat this process throughout the track. At the end of the exercise, ask students if any of their guesses were correct and, if so, why they chose that word. Remember not to comment on the accuracy of their guesses during the exercise – the goal isn't to get everything right, but to concentrate on the language and topic in order to make guessing possible.

Reading

Using things you know to help you read

Asking students to talk about what they know and to use their background knowledge of a topic before they read a text not only encourages them to engage with the content but also helps them predict the meaning of the language they're going to read. They will rely on their knowledge of the content rather than on their linguistic knowledge and will be more likely to be able to use contextual clues to help them figure out the meanings of words they don't know.
It encourages them to read and engage with the text as a whole rather than concentrating on individual words and structures.

Classroom activities to promote this include asking students to predict what they're going to read by looking at the title of a text or giving students discussion questions directly related to the content of the text.

Understanding the main ideas

In order to understand the main ideas, a reader uses text details as well as existing knowledge to think about what the main message might be. Remind students that at this stage it is not necessary for them to understand everything in a reading text; they should read quickly to identify related details. The reader combines all the evidence to decide on the general topic and the main ideas in the text.

Taking notes

Taking notes is often not an easy task for students with this level of English, as it requires a fairly deep understanding of the text in order to understand which information is important. Students are often tempted to copy sentences, as they're unsure which information they'll need. Certain strategies can help students take effective notes from a reading text:

- Having a purpose for taking notes (e.g., for a test, important information to tell parents). This will encourage students to think about what they need the notes for in the future and which information they need from the text.
- Reading the text at least once before they start so that they become familiar with the text, any unfamiliar language, and the key points in the text.
- Reading the text and then trying to remember the key points in order to summarize them orally. This will encourage students to pay attention to the text and focus on the main ideas.
- Pointing out that students need to write only the words that carry meaning; they don't need to copy complete sentences. These words are often names, places, dates, numbers, and possibly adjectives. Give students question prompts to help them: *What?, Where?, When?, Why?, How?*

Jigsaw reading

For longer pieces of reading, put students in pairs and give them a section each to read. When they have finished reading, encourage students to tell each other what they have read and to ask each other questions. Then allow time for them to read the full text.

Teaching pronunciation

IPA

English is not a phonetic language. The alphabet that we use to write English has 26 letters, but in American English there are approximately 44 speech sounds. To represent each sound, we use a set of phonetic symbols called the International Phonetic Alphabet (IPA). It is not necessary to have students memorize the IPA, but it is a good idea to help them become familiar with the IPA symbols that are used in the Student's Book.

Intro Question intonation

There is final rising intonation for a Yes/No question:

Are you Canadian?

and final falling intonation for *Wh-* questions:

What's your name?

Intro The /iz/ sound

When a word ends in sibilant or hissing sounds such as *-ches, -ses, -shes, -zes,* or *-xes*, the *-es* ending is pronounced as a separate syllable.

This is because these sounds are so similar to the *-s* ending that the ending must be pronounced as a separate syllable in order to be clearly heard.

Intro Long and short vowel sounds

Some languages do not have a distinction between short and long vowels. Speakers of these languages often stretch all vowel sounds and confuse pairs of short and long English vowel sounds like the short vowel sound in *ship* /ɪ/ and the long vowel sound in *sheep* /i/. The vowel sound /i/ is a long *e* (as in *eat*) and you can help students say it by asking them to smile when saying it, as if they're having a photo taken and saying *Cheese!*

Intro *Was/wasn't* – weak and strong forms

There are two different ways of pronouncing *was*, the strong and weak form:

In affirmative sentences and questions *was* is pronounced as the weak form /wəz/:

He was at the park on Saturday.

/hiwəzætðəpɑrkɔnsætərdeɪ/

Was he at the park on Saturday?

/wəzhiætðəpɑrkɔnsætərdeɪ/

However, in short answers the strong form /wɑz/ is used:

Yes, he was.

/jeshiwɑz/

In negative sentences and short answers the strong form is used. We usually don't pronounce the final /t/:

He wasn't at the park on Saturday.

/hiwɑzənæðəpɑrkɔnsætərdeɪ/

No, he wasn't.

/noʊhiwɑzən/

Intro The /θ/ sound

Some students may have difficulty pronouncing the /θ/ sound (e.g., ***th**irty* /ˈθɜrti/). Ask students to touch their top front teeth with their tongues and blow softly so that they can feel how the sound is formed. Drill the pronunciation of words with the /θ/ sound as a whole class.

Intro Words ending in *-ed*

There are three ways of pronouncing the *-ed* ending.

	Pronunciation of *-ed*	Examples
Unvoiced verb ending	/t/	*wash / washed*
Voiced verb ending	/d/	*play / played*
Verb ending in /t/ or /d/	/ɪd/	*start / started*

It is not always easy to distinguish between voiced and unvoiced endings; however, by placing your hand on your throat, you can feel the vibration of a voiced sound. It is not so important for students to clearly pronounce a /t/ or /d/ past tense ending, as native speakers often do not pronounce these endings clearly. However, it is important for students to learn when to use the /ɪd/ ending and when not to use it.

Pronunciation Mountain

This is a simple and effective way to drill any list of vocabulary. Students enjoy the competitive nature of the activity and benefit from repeating each word multiple times. You can play it with words from the vocabulary you have studied in class or at the end of the class with words you have noticed students mispronouncing throughout the class.

- Put a list of about 10 words on the board. Put the word you think is easiest to pronounce at the bottom of the list and the one that is the most difficult at the top.
- Divide the class into teams of four or five.
- Set a time limit of two minutes for the teams to practice saying the words together.
- When you say *Go!* the first team must all say the word at the bottom of the list together. If they pronounce the word correctly, they move up to the next word. They continue moving up the list until the team, or someone on the team, pronounces one of the words wrong.
- Then it is the next team's turn, and they start from the bottom of the list again and keep moving up until they get a word wrong. Each time a team makes a mistake, they have to start from the bottom of the list when it is their turn again.
- The game continues until one team reaches the top of the list and wins the game.

GAMES

Broken Telephone

This game introduces the idea of communication breakdown and the importance of good pronunciation when talking on the phone.

- Divide the class into groups of about 10 students from the front to the back of the classroom.
- Give one student in each group a sentence to memorize (e.g., *Grandpa has five chickens, and my brother has a black horse*).
- Each student whispers the sentence to the next student and so on, until it reaches the last person in the group.
- The last person in the group then says the sentence back to the first person, who indicates how it has changed.

The winning group is the one in which the last student gets the sentence correct or has the closest sentence to the original.

Memory

This is a game that is traditionally played with playing cards. The cards are spread out face down, either randomly or in rows, and the players take turns picking up two cards. If the cards have the same number, the player keeps them and takes another turn. If the cards don't match, the player returns the cards and it's the next player's turn. The winner is the player with the most cards at the end of the game.

This game can be adapted to cover many language areas. For example, you could have a set of transportation words on cards (e.g., *bus*, *train*, *car*, etc.) with corresponding picture cards. The players then have to match a word and the appropriate picture card. Another possibility is to have simple past forms and their corresponding base verb forms.

Picture Dictation

This is a fun team game and great for more visual learners. To play the game, you need to have words, phrases, or sentences written on pieces of paper or cards.

Each team has one minute to take turns coming to the board, taking a card, and drawing the word, phrase, or sentence for their team to guess. The team who has guessed the most words at the end of the game wins.

Find Someone Who ...

This game is good for question practice and for practicing a range of new grammar and vocabulary points.

- Prepare a worksheet with the statement *Find someone who ...* at the top, and underneath write a number of endings (e.g., *... has two brothers*, *... has a TV in his or her room*, etc.). This works best if you use information that you know is true of at least one student.
- Explain that students have to ask each other questions and try to find a different person for each ending. Model the task by asking students the first question: *Do you have two brothers?* When someone says yes, write his or her name next to the ending.
- Tell students that the objective is to find one name for each statement. Set a time limit of five minutes and have students mingle and ask questions. After five minutes, stop the activity and invite students to say what they found out about the group.

Chain Stories

At this level, this game can be used to practice the simple past for telling a story. It is described here as a writing activity, but it could also be done orally.

- Write a sentence on the board to start the chain (e.g., *I saw her at the station*) and invite a student to come to the board and write a sentence that could follow it: *I saw her at the station. She looked at me.*
- Then invite other students to come to the board and add a sentence. If it is a small class, you could have students take two turns.
- Stop the activity when everyone has added a sentence. As a follow-up activity, remove the story from the board and ask students to rewrite it in their notebooks from memory.

Snowman

To elicit a word or phrase or to give extra practice in spelling, write short lines for each letter of the word or phrase on the board and invite students to guess letters. For each incorrect guess, draw a part of a snowman: one circle for the head, one for the body, then two arms, three buttons, a hat, two eyes, and a smile.

Note that you can play the game in reverse: draw the snowman to start with, then erase a part each time a student guesses incorrectly until the snowman disappears (or "melts").

Vocabulary Tennis

This is a great game to review different sets of vocabulary. You will need a ball for this (or a wadded-up piece of paper).

- Divide the class into two teams. Ask them to sit in two lines on either side of the classroom, across from each other, so that everyone on each team is facing someone from the other team.
- Explain that you will give them a category (e.g., food). The first person from team one must say a word that belongs to that category and then throw the ball to someone on the other team (it doesn't have to be the person across from the thrower).
- The person with the ball now says another word and throws the ball back to someone on the other team. This continues until a word is repeated or someone takes longer than five seconds to say a word. In these cases, the points go to the other team and the teacher gives another category.
- The game can be scored by giving a point for each round won or like a game of tennis, in which case the first team to reach 40 is the winner.

Alphabet Race

- Divide the class into two teams and divide the board in half. Write the letters of the alphabet down each side of the board (don't include *Q*, *X*, or *Z*).
  Set a time limit of three minutes for students to take turns coming up to the board and writing a word beginning with each letter of the alphabet.
- Explain that if both teams have the same word for the same letter, it doesn't count as a point. This will discourage copying.
  At the end of the three minutes, count how many words each team has correct. The team with the most correct words is the winner.
- This game can be adapted to review vocabulary learned in class (e.g., names of stores, verbs, clothes).

USING THE *MOVE BEYOND* TEACHER'S EDITION

This Teacher's Edition is a valuable and practical resource. With its clear and comprehensive teaching notes, audio scripts and answer keys, background notes, and extra features, it will help you plan and deliver impactful, well-paced, and memorable lessons.

The topic, content, and lesson objectives of each unit are clearly presented.

The target language, functions, and stages of each lesson are outlined, with suggested timings for each stage shown visually to help you pace your lesson. The darker gray shading shows the part of the lesson already completed, and the lighter gray shows the amount of time allocated for each stage.

The Get started feature provides an activity to start the lesson and is an opportunity to recycle language and prepare students for the lesson. These warm-ups do not require additional preparation or materials.

Activities that recycle language are labeled with the recycle icon.

Clear and concise procedural notes maximize the Student's Book material.

3 ANIMAL MAGIC

IN THE PICTURE Adopt a pet

Talk about pets

Pages 30–31

STAGE	TIME	FOCUS
GET STARTED		Play a game to practice saying letters of the alphabet and lead in to the topic of the unit.
WORK WITH WORDS		Review parts of the body. Learn and practice using vocabulary for pets. Practice pronunciation of the short /ɪ/ sound. Watch a video of animals, write the names of the animals, and count them.
WRITE AND SPEAK		Talk about pets.

Get started

In order to lead in to the topic of the unit – animals – in a fun way, play a game of *Snowman* (see Games, page 29) with famous cartoon and movie animals. First, ask students to think of a famous animal (e.g., Mickey Mouse, Pingu, etc.), and then play once as a class to make sure students understand the game. Divide the class into groups of four to play the game, circulating and helping students with pronouncing the letters as necessary. Stop the activity after five minutes and ask students what famous animals they thought of. Elicit the types of animals they are (or tell them) and write them on the board (e.g., *mouse, penguin*, etc.).

WORK WITH WORDS Pet animals

1 RECALL

- Ask a student to read the instructions aloud. Refer students to the example and elicit another example.
- Divide the class into pairs and set a time limit of one minute for them to write the parts of the body.
- Call on students to share their answers with the class.
- Ask students to do the Work with Words task on page 58.

SUGGESTED ANSWERS
back eye face foot head leg mouth nose

2a

- Point out that the animals in the pictures are pets and elicit the meaning of *pet*.
- Read the instructions aloud and set a time limit of two minutes for the task.
- After two minutes, let students compare their answers in pairs, but don't check them at this stage.

2b 40

- Play the track for students to listen and check their answers to Exercise 2a. Then call on students to share their answers with the class.
- Play the rest of the track for students to listen and repeat the words.

ANSWERS 40
bird a cat ... horse d ... mouse
bird cat ... rabbit turtle

Extra activity
To give students extra practice in saying the words, divide the class into A/B pairs. Tell Student As to close their books and try to recall all the animals in the same order as they are in the book. Tell Student Bs to listen and if Student A makes a mistake, to switch roles.

MOVE BEYOND FOR TEACHERS
Adopt a pet

In many countries, it's now very popular to adopt a pet rather than buying one. Organizations and charities often have websites where you can find the right pet for you. This means that animals that might otherwise be homeless can be matched with a new owner. In this lesson, the text and pictures show a similar website. If you have access to the internet in your classroom, you might want to show your students an authentic website and have students search for animals they'd like to adopt.

3a

- Point out that the pictures are from a website about pets and refer students to the tablet with the *Adopt a Pet* website.
- Read the instructions aloud and have students read the first description and match it to an animal.
- Check ideas as a class. Then have students match the rest of the descriptions to animals.
- Let students compare their answers in pairs, but don't check them at this point.

3b 41
- Play the track for students to listen and check their answers to Exercise 3a.

ANSWERS / AUDIO SCRIPT 41
1 horse
2 dog
3 chicken
4 cat
5 bird

4a 42
- Ask a student to read the instructions aloud. Refer students to the example and remind them to use the animals from Exercise 2a.
- Play the track for students to listen and write the animals.
- Let students compare their answers in pairs before you check them as a class.

ANSWERS / AUDIO SCRIPT 42
2 fish 3 turtle 4 mouse 5 hamster

1
Julia: This is my pet rabbit, Harvey. He has very, very big ears. He's three years old, and he's a very happy rabbit.
2
Brian: Um ... this one's name is Happy, and that one's Grumpy. Where's Smiley? Ah! There he is! I have a lot of fish. It's hard to remember their names.
3
Karen: This is Terry. My pet turtle's eight years old. Look! He has small eyes and a big mouth. He loves the water!
4
Leo: So her name is Minnie ... you know, Minnie's the name of Mickey Mouse's girlfriend? She's very small. She likes to sit on my hand. She's a good mouse.
5
Nicky: I think it's a Russian hamster. It doesn't have a name. It's brown, and it has a black line down its back.

4b 42
- Read the instructions aloud and give students a minute to read the questions.
- Play the track for students to listen and answer the questions.
- Let students compare their answers in pairs before you check them as a class.

ANSWERS / AUDIO SCRIPT 42
2 Julia's pet has big ears
3 Karen's pet has small eyes.
4 Nicky's pet doesn't have a name.
See Exercise 4a for audio script.

Alternative procedure
Before playing the track, you could ask students if they remember the answers and ask them to discuss them in pairs. Invite students to share their ideas with the class. Then play the track to check their answers.

5a 43 PRONOUNCE
- Read the instructions aloud and model the /ɪ/ sound. Point out that it's a short sound. (See Teaching Tips, *Long and short vowel sounds*, page 28.)
- Play the track for students to listen and repeat the words.

AUDIO SCRIPT 43
See Student's Book, page 30, for audio script.

b 44
- Play the track for students to listen and repeat the words.

AUDIO SCRIPT 44
See Student's Book, page 30, for audio script.

Extra activity
For further practice of the /ɪ/ sound, write the following short conversations that recycle vocabulary from Unit 1 on the board:
- *Who visits Pittsburgh?*
- *Tourists visit Pittsburgh.*
- *Where's the little dog?*
- *In the living room.*
- *It isn't in the living room.*
- *Oh! It's in the kitchen.*

Invite students to come to the boa[rd] ... /ɪ/ sounds. Give students a couple ... the conversations in pairs, and the[n] ... present them for the class.

6 THE MOVING PICTURE
- Ask a student to read the instructions aloud.
- Play the video for students to watch and write the animals they see.
- Play the video again for students to watch and count how many animals there are.
- Let students compare their answers in pairs before you check them as a class.

ANSWERS / VIDEO SCRIPT
There are 10.
1 fish (two) 2 cat (one) 3 dogs (five) 4 hamste[r] ...
5 horses (four) 6 mice (two) 7 birds (three)
8 turtle (one) 9 rabbit (one) 10 chickens (12)
There is no dialog in this video.

WRITE AND SPEAK

7a
- Read the instructions aloud and model the task by choosing an animal and writing some notes on the board.
- Give students two minutes to complete the form.

7b
- Read the instructions al[oud] ... useful phrases. Model t[he] ... to your notes on the boa[rd] ... pet.
- Divid[e] ... their pets. A ... partners' pets so they c... time limit of three minut[es].
- Monitor and note good u... feedback at the end of t...
- Invite students to tell th... Then give feedback and correct errors.

MOVE BEYOND
Ask students to do the Words & Beyond exercise on page 58.

The optional extra activities provide ideas for extending the lesson and offering additional practice.

Complete scripts for the Moving Picture videos are embedded in the lesson notes.

Alternative procedure suggestions are provided for selected exercises, offering a different approach to teaching the Student's Book content. These alternatives appeal to different learning styles and abilities.

Activity suggestions for fast finishers are provided throughout the lessons.

Answer keys and audio scripts are embedded within the teaching notes.

Other features

The Teacher's Edition also contains:

Procedural notes for the Unit Reviews and Progress Checks
Full and detailed notes are given for the Unit Reviews and Progress Checks in the Student's Book.

Workbook answer keys and audio scripts
At the back of the Teacher's Edition, answer keys and audio scripts are given for the corresponding Workbook.

Teaching Tips
Pages 24–29 of the Teacher's Edition provide useful tips on classroom management and teaching vocabulary, grammar, skills, and pronunciation, as well as using games in the classroom.

Homework
Task-based homework is provided at the end of every lesson and is related to the topic or skill of the lesson.

Background information
Useful and interesting background information on specific lesson topics is provided in the Move Beyond for Teachers feature to help with the presentation of the content.

S GET READY: IT'S MY PARTY

STAGE	TIME	FOCUS
GET STARTED		Play a game to help students and teachers learn names quickly.
THINK AND READ		Talk about costume parties. Read a story and find out Emily's favorite color.
RECALL		Recycle vocabulary to talk about numbers 1–20 and colors. Review the structure of *be*, subject pronouns, and possessive adjectives. Practice making introductions. Write an invitation to a party.
THINK AND READ		Read a story to find out who a person in a costume is.
RECALL		Recycle vocabulary to talk about numbers 20–100, days of the week, and months. Review the structure of *be* in negatives, questions, and short answers. Review question words. Practice asking for contact information.

Get started

Play a game of *Quick-fire Ball* to help you and your students learn each other's names quickly. Start by saying your name: *My name's … What's your name?* and throwing a ball or scrunched up piece of paper to a student. That student responds by saying his or her name; for example, *My name's Sara Johnson. What's your name?* The student then throws the ball to another student, and so on.

HELLO! *Pages 4–5*

THINK AND READ

1 01

- Draw students' attention to the party invitation. Elicit from students what *costume* means. If they know, invite them to explain it to the class in English (*special clothes you wear to a party to look like famous people, characters, etc.*). Encourage students to say what the costume theme is for this party (*Wear your favorite color*).
- Ask some simple questions about the invitation; for example, *What day is the party? What time does it start? Who's having the party? Where do they live? Can you go with a friend?*
- Focus students' attention on the story. Play the track for students to read the story and find out what Emily's favorite color is. (See Teaching Tips, *Recorded reading texts*, page 27.)
- Explain to students that Emily and Leo arrive at the party in regular clothes and change into their costumes when they arrive at the party. Call on a student to give the answer.
- Ask students to find Emily and Leo in the picture. (*Emily is in the banana costume; Leo is walking out of the door.*)

ANSWER / AUDIO SCRIPT 01

Emily's favorite color is yellow.

See Student's Book, pages 4–5, for audio script.

Extra activity

Have students work in pairs to find all the names of the people in the story, and then identify whether they are girls or boys. (*Girls: Karen, Lucy, Maria, Emily; Boys: Leo, Eric, Ben*)

2

- Ask students to read the story again in preparation for doing the exercises that follow.

RECALL

1a NUMBERS 1–20 02

- Draw students' attention to the example.
- Encourage students to work in pairs to complete the numbers with *a*, *e*, *i*, *o*, and *u*.
- Play the track for students to listen and repeat. Remind students of the syllable stress in the teens (e.g., thir<u>teen</u>).

ANSWERS / AUDIO SCRIPT 02

2 two 3 three 4 four 5 five 6 six 7 seven
8 eight 9 nine 10 ten 11 eleven 12 twelve
13 thirteen 14 fourteen 15 fifteen 16 sixteen
17 seventeen 18 eighteen 19 nineteen 20 twenty

one two three four five six seven eight nine
ten eleven twelve thirteen fourteen fifteen sixteen
seventeen eighteen nineteen twenty

Fast finishers

Ask fast finishers to choose three numbers from the list that are important to them (*birthday*, *street number*, *favorite number*, etc.). Then have them work in pairs and ask and answer questions about the numbers, for example:

A: What's your favorite number?
B: Fourteen because my birthday is March 14th.

1b

- Divide the class into A/B pairs. (See Teaching Tips, *Pairwork*, page 24.)
- Tell Student As to say a number from 1 to 20 and Student Bs to close their books and write the number in letters.
- Encourage Student As to check the number.
- Ask students to switch roles and repeat the procedure.

Alternative procedure: more confident classes

Ask students to choose five numbers to test their partners.

2a INTRODUCTIONS

- Go over the example with the class.
- Ask students to write the words in the correct order.

2b 03

- Play the track for students to listen and check their answers.
- Play the track again and ask students to repeat the sentences, paying particular attention to the contracted forms.

ANSWERS / AUDIO SCRIPT 03

See underlining in audio script.

Maria: Hi. <u>I'm Maria</u>.
Eric: Hello. <u>My name's Eric</u>.
Maria: <u>This is Mark</u>.

Extra activity
Have students practice the conversation in pairs, substituting the names in the conversation with real information about themselves.

3 PRONOUNS AND POSSESSIVE ADJECTIVES
- Ask students to complete the table with the correct subject pronouns and possessive adjectives.
- Circulate and monitor to give help as necessary.
- Go around the class, calling on students to give the answers. (See Teaching Tips, *Checking answers 1*, page 24.)

ANSWERS
3 Your 4 He 5 It 6 Our

Alternative procedure: less confident classes
After completing Exercise 3, encourage students to take turns testing each other in pairs. Explain that Student As should read aloud one word from one side of the table while Student Bs keep their books closed and say the corresponding word from the other side of the table. When they finish, ask them to switch roles.

4 04
- Before playing the track, ask students to complete Karen's sentences with words from the table in Exercise 3.
- Play the track for students to listen and check their answers. Remind them to use capital letters at the beginning of a sentence.

ANSWERS / AUDIO SCRIPT 04
2 his 3 They 4 Your 5 Its
See Student's Book, page 7, for audio script.

Alternative procedure: more confident classes
Encourage students to change all the names and nouns in sentences 1–5 and to make any necessary changes to the subject pronouns and possessive adjectives; for example, *1 Ben's here with his friend, Chloe.* Call on several students to give their answers for each of the sentences.

5 COLORS 05
- Ask students to match the colors to the words.
- Call on students around the class to give the answers.
- Play the track for students to listen and repeat.

ANSWERS / AUDIO SCRIPT 05
black a blue d brown i green e orange j pink c
purple b red h white g yellow f
black blue brown green orange pink purple
red white yellow

Extra activity
Ask students to work in pairs to find one thing in the classroom for each color. Write some example sentences on the board; for example, *Marco's T-shirt is blue; That chair is orange.*

Extra activity
Use this opportunity to recycle the pronunciation of the letters of the alphabet. Write the letters on the board like this:

/eɪ/	/i/	/e/	/aɪ/	/oʊ/	/u/	/ɑr/
A H	B C	F L M	I Y	O	Q U	R
J K	D E	N S X			W	
	G P					
	T V					
	Z					

Drill the letters chorally column by column and point out (in L1 if necessary) that they're grouped by vowel sound, and that the symbols at the top are the phonetic symbols for the different vowel sounds. Then ask students to take turns spelling the colors in Exercise 5 to each other.

6a *BE*
- Ask students to complete the sentences with *am*, *are*, or *is*.
- Let students compare their answers in pairs before playing the track for students to check answers.

6b 06
- Play the track for students to listen and check.
- Point out to students that contractions are not usually used when there is more than one subject, for example, *Chloe and Kayla are ~~'re~~ really good friends.*

ANSWERS / AUDIO SCRIPT 06
2 are 3 is 4 am 5 is 6 are 7 is 8 are
See Student's Book, page 7, for audio script.

Fast finishers
Encourage fast finishers to read the conversation aloud in pairs. Then have students switch roles and repeat the procedure.

7 HAVE A PARTY
- Ask students to write an invitation to their party. Refer them to the invitation in the story and encourage them to think of their own theme.

Extra activity
Ask students to work in groups of four or six. Tell them they're at a party and have them introduce themselves and a partner to the other people in the group. Go around the class and monitor the activity, offering feedback where necessary.

AT THE PARTY *Pages 6–7*

THINK AND READ

1 07
- Play the track and ask students to read the story to find out who Maximus is.
- Call on a student to give the answer.

ANSWER / AUDIO SCRIPT 07
Maximus is really Leo.
See Student's Book, pages 6–7, for audio script.

2
- Ask students to read the story again in preparation for doing the exercises that follow.

RECALL

1 NUMBERS 20–100 ▶08

- Ask students to match the numbers to the words.
- Play the track for students to listen and repeat, paying special attention to the /θ/ sound in *thirty* as some students may find this difficult. (See Teaching Tips, *The /θ/ sound*, page 28.)
- Point out and practice the different syllable stress in *thirteen* (through nineteen) and *thirty* (through ninety).

ANSWERS / AUDIO SCRIPT ▶08

20 twenty 30 thirty 40 forty 50 fifty 60 *sixty*
70 seventy 80 eighty 90 ninety 100 one hundred

twenty thirty forty fifty sixty seventy eighty
ninety one hundred

Extra activity

Divide students into groups of three or four to play the game *Buzz* described on the Student's Book, page 6. Vary it by using multiples of different numbers. Make it more challenging by using two numbers; for example, students say *Buzz* for multiples of 5, *Fizz* for multiples of 2, and *Fizz Buzz* for numbers that are multiples of both 2 and 5.

2a DAYS OF THE WEEK ▶09

- Ask students to write the days of the week in order.
- Play the track for students to check their answers.
- Play the track again for students to listen and repeat.

ANSWERS / AUDIO SCRIPT ▶09

Monday *Tuesday* Wednesday Thursday
Friday Saturday Sunday

2b

- Divide the class into pairs. Ask students to close their books and write the days.
- Ask students to open their books and check their spelling.

3a MONTHS

- Divide the class into pairs and have them decide on the correct order for the months.
- Ask students to write the months in the correct order.
- Elicit the months from different pairs of students.

3b ▶10

- Play the track for students to check their answers.
- Play the track again for students to listen and repeat.

ANSWERS / AUDIO SCRIPT ▶10

January *February* March April May June July
August September October November December

Extra activity

Divide the class into groups of five or six. Encourage students to play the party game with the months. Refer students to the instructions on how to play the game in the story. In a less confident class, play the game as a whole class first.

4 *BE:* NEGATIVE, QUESTIONS, AND SHORT ANSWERS ▶11

- Ask students to complete the conversation with the words in the box.
- Play the track for students to check their answers.
- Play the track again for students to listen and repeat. (See Teaching Tips, *Question intonation*, page 28.)

ANSWERS / AUDIO SCRIPT ▶11

2 isn't 3 'm not 4 Are 5 am 6 aren't

See Student's Book, page 6, for audio script.

Alternative procedure: less confident classes

Write the verb forms below on the board and ask students to write example sentences for each form. Walk around and monitor, helping as necessary.

***be* negative**

I'm not (am not) / you/we/they aren't (are not) / he/she/it isn't (is not)

***be* questions**

Am I … ? / Are you/we/they … ? / Is he/she/it … ?

***be* short answers**

Yes, I am. / Yes, you/we/they are. / Yes, he/she/it is. / No, I'm not. / No, you/we/they aren't. / No, he/she/it isn't.

5a QUESTION WORDS

- Ask students to match the question words to the pictures.

ANSWERS

2 What? c 3 Where? a 4 When? b 5 How old? d

5b ▶12

- Ask students to complete the conversation with question words.
- Play the track for students to listen and check their answers.

ANSWERS / AUDIO SCRIPT ▶12

2 When 3 Who 4 What

See Student's Book, page 9, for audio script.

Fast finishers

Encourage fast finishers to read the conversation aloud in pairs, paying attention to the falling intonation in *Wh-* questions. Then have students switch roles and repeat the procedure.

6 PHONE CONTACTS

- Divide the class into pairs. Have them ask questions and complete the contact information for each other.
- Remind students that we usually say phone numbers in single digits and that when 0 is in a phone number, it's pronounced *oh* (e.g., *482-0980 four – eight – two, oh – nine – eight – oh*).

Homework

Ask students to make an odd-one-out quiz from the vocabulary and grammar in this unit. Model an example for the class; for example, *October Monday September June* (Answer – *Monday. The others are months*). Have students write at least three examples to test a partner at the beginning of the next class. The partner must select the odd one out and justify his or her choice.

ME

IN THE PICTURE My things

Talk about your things

Pages 8–9

STAGE	TIME	FOCUS
GET STARTED		Review the letters of the alphabet.
WORK WITH WORDS		Review and brainstorm common nouns and categorize them. Practice spelling words. Watch a video and write the categories in the correct order.
WRITE AND SPEAK		Talk about your favorite words.

Get started

Review the letters of the alphabet by starting with the letter *a* and calling on students to say the letters that follow. Then focus students on the pronunciation of the letters by writing the phonemes /eɪ/ /i/ /e/ /aɪ/ /oʊ/ /u/ /ɑr/ on the board. Model and drill the sounds. Then ask students to work in pairs and decide which of the sounds the letters of the alphabet correspond to. Then invite different students to come to the board and add the letters under the correct sound.

ANSWER

See Extra activity for Student's Book, page 5, Exercise 5, on page 33.

WORK WITH WORDS Things

1

- Direct students' attention to the pictures on pages 8–9. Then go over the phrases in the PHRASE BYTES box.
- Divide the class into pairs.
- Tell students to take turns asking and answering questions to try to name as many of the things in the pictures as possible. Remind them to use the phrases in the PHRASE BYTES box.
- While students are doing the task, circulate and help with pronunciation as necessary.
- Do not confirm answers at this point, as answers will be checked in Exercise 2b.

2a

- Ask students to match the things in the pictures to the words in the box. Do not check answers at this point, as students will listen and check in the next exercise.

2b ▶13

- Play the track for students to listen and check their answers. You may want to point out that *bike* is a short form of *bicycle*.
- Continue the track for students to listen and repeat the words in the box.

ANSWERS / AUDIO SCRIPT ▶13

1 backpack 2 soccer ball 3 notebook 4 orange
5 sandwich 6 sunglasses 7 T-shirt
8 website 9 game console 10 bike 11 phone
12 ice cream 13 jeans 14 laptop 15 car

backpack bike car game console ice cream jeans
laptop notebook orange phone sandwich soccer ball
sunglasses T-shirt website

3a

- Have students read the instructions and check that they understand what the categories are. (See Teaching Tips, *Word lists*, page 25.)
- Do an example with the class to check that students understand what to do. Have students look at the picture of the backpack and elicit that it goes in the *school* category. Point out that some of the words may fit into more than one category, for example, *laptop*.
- Divide the class into pairs and set a time limit of three minutes for the activity.

3b

- Call on students to share their answers for each category with the class. Ask other students whether they agree or disagree and accept any answers that are possible.

SUGGESTED ANSWERS

Clothes	Food	Games
jeans sunglasses T-shirt	ice cream sandwich orange	soccer ball game console
School	**Technology**	**Transportation**
backpack notebook	laptop phone website	bike car

3c ▶14

- Play the track for students to listen, check their answers, and repeat the words. Point out the stressed syllables in the more problematic words (e.g., *technology*, *transportation*). You could also point out that *clothes* has only one syllable.

> **AUDIO SCRIPT** ▶14
> See answers to Exercise 3b for audio script.

4a

- Go over the instructions and elicit some examples of other words for the categories.
- Divide the class into small groups and explain that this is a race to think of as many words as possible for each category. Set a time limit of three minutes. While students are working, draw the chart on the board and write in the words from Exercise 3.

4b

- Focus on each category in turn and find out which group has the most words. Ask a student from the group with the most words to come to the board and add the words. Then invite other groups to call out any other words they can add to the class list. Ask students to copy the chart with all of the words into their notebooks. Remind them to be careful of spelling.

5 THE MOVING PICTURE ▶

- Ask students to watch the video and write the categories in the order they see them.
- Let students compare their answers in pairs before you check them as a class.

> **ANSWERS / VIDEO SCRIPT**
> 1 Food 2 School 3 Clothes 4 Transportation
> 5 Technology 6 Games
> There is no dialog in this video.

6a ▶15 PRONOUNCE

- Ask students to listen to the alphabet rap and repeat the letters.

> **AUDIO SCRIPT** ▶15
> A B C D E F G H I J K L M N O P Q R S T U V W X Y Z

6b

- Explain the instructions. Then call on two students to read the model conversation aloud.
- Divide the class into A and B pairs and set a time limit of four minutes, asking students to switch roles halfway through.
- Circulate and make a note of any problems for feedback at the end of the activity.
- Invite students to say how many words they guessed before their partner finished spelling them.

WRITE AND SPEAK

7

- Read the instructions aloud and give students examples of your favorite words for some of the categories. Try to make the words interesting but not too obscure to avoid having to illustrate or explain each one.
- Ask students to write their favorite words for each category in their notebooks. Encourage stronger students to close their Student's Book and write the words from memory.
- Refer students to the useful phrases in the PHRASE BYTES box, and then model the task by inviting students to ask you questions from the PHRASE BYTES box. Encourage students to extend their answers; for example, *My favorite word for games is "video game." I have a lot of video games!*
- Divide the class into pairs and set a time limit of three minutes for students to do the task.
- Invite students to tell the class about their favorite words.

MOVE BEYOND

Ask students to do the Words & Beyond exercise on page 56.

> **Homework**
>
> Ask students to add 10 more words to their word lists from the Work with Words exercise on page 56. Explain that each word should begin with a different letter, and remind students to write the L1 translation for each word. In the next class, have students compare their words in small groups and say what each word means. Ask students to give an example or two of their most interesting words and to check the meanings of any difficult words with the class.

READING Worldwide words

Read an article from a book *Page 10*

STAGE	TIME	FOCUS
GET STARTED		Review words from pages 8–9 and practice saying letters of the alphabet.
SPEAK AND READ		Translate words into your language and say which ones are similar in your language (reading subskill). Read an article from a book about international words. Categorize sections of the article and decide which words in the article are international.
REACT		Talk about your favorite international words. Make a phrasebook of international words.

Get started

Play *Snowman* (see Games, page 29) with the lesser known words from pages 8–9. This will provide further practice for saying the letters of the alphabet and reviewing the words from the previous lesson.

SPEAK AND READ

1

- Call on a student to read the instructions aloud and have students repeat the words in the box to practice pronunciation. Highlight the stress in *café*, *coffee*, *hotel*, *music*, *radio*, and *taxi*.
- Refer students to the PHRASE BYTES box and model the task, eliciting words from students to complete the phrases.
- Divide the class into pairs and set a time limit of three minutes for the task. Remind students to work together and to use the useful phrases.
- Invite students to share their ideas with the class and ask other students if they agree or disagree.

2 ▶16

- Write the word *article* on the board and ask students where they can read one (e.g., *in a magazine, newspaper, book, or online*). Tell students what articles you like to read (e.g., *I read articles about sports and politics*), and ask them what articles they like to read.
- Ask students to look at the pictures and say what they can see.
- Ask students to read the beginning of the article and answer the question. Don't play the audio at this point. It is an extra feature, and a suggestion for using it is included at the end of the lesson.
- Choose a student to answer the question for the class. Point out that many words that refer to technology are international.

SUGGESTED ANSWER
An international word is the same or very similar in many different languages.

3

- Have a student read the instructions and the words in the box aloud. Check that students understand the two new categories, *Drinks* and *Places*.
- Reassure students that they don't have to understand all the words at this point, but that they should underline any new words.
- Set a time limit of three minutes for students to match the sections of the article to the categories.
- Let students compare their answers in pairs before you check them as a class. Discuss any new words from the article.

ANSWERS
1 Transportation 2 Technology 3 Drinks 4 Food
5 Places

Fast finishers
Ask fast finishers to cover the text and write down from memory the international words that are mentioned for each category.

4

- Have students read the article again and then decide which words from Exercise 1 are international.
- Ask students to compare their answers before you check them as a class.
- It may be argued that *train* and *bus* are also international words (e.g., *bus* is commonly used in European languages), so be prepared for differences of opinion and encourage students to give their opinions.

ANSWERS
café, coffee, hotel, music, radio, taxi

REACT

5

- Read the instructions aloud and ask students to choose from any of the words in the lesson.
- Give students a couple of minutes to choose their words. Then divide the class into pairs and ask students to compare their words with their partners.
- Encourage students to explain their choices; for example, *I like the word "café" because I like small restaurants.*
- Do a quick survey to find out which are the class's favorite words.

MOVE BEYOND

Suggest to students that they start a new page in their notebooks for international words.

Ask students to write down all the international words from the lesson and to try to think of more words for each category.

Have students compare their phrasebooks with a partner and include any words from their partner's list.

Invite students to share the new words on their list with the class.

Recorded reading text 16

In order to give extra listening practice, have students listen to the audio rather than read the text. As students may find this more difficult when listening to the five sections, play the sections one at a time and have students call out the category that they've heard. Explain that they do not have to try to understand any details, but should simply try to identify the topic, or category, of each section.

Homework

Ask students to work alone and make a poster of international words for the classroom. Ask them to find or draw pictures for at least 10 of the international words and to write the words next to the pictures. Display the posters around the classroom in the next class and invite students to move around the classroom and decide which poster is their favorite.

GRAMMAR Plural nouns; *a/an, the*

Talk about one or more things

Page 11

STAGE	TIME	FOCUS
GET STARTED		Play a game of *Pronunciation Mountain* to practice word stress and review international words.
READ		Read a social networking site about someone's likes and dislikes.
STUDY		Read grammar explanations of noun plurals and articles and complete examples.
PRACTICE		Practice writing plural nouns and decide when to use an article (*a/an, the*) or no article.
WRITE AND SPEAK		Talk about your likes and dislikes.

Get started

Play a game of *Pronunciation Mountain* (see Teaching Tips, page 28) to review pronunciation of the international words from page 10. Choose 10 words and include some that require students to think about word stress (e.g., *hotel*, *coffee*). At the end of the game, ask students which words are more difficult to pronounce and suggest that they review and practice them regularly.

READ Grammar in context

1

- Have students look at the "Social Scene" text and ask them *Where do you see a text like this?* (*on a social networking site, e.g., Facebook*). Point out the thumbs up and thumbs down icons as students will probably be familiar with these for representing likes and dislikes.
- Before having students read the text, elicit the meanings of any words they may not know (e.g., *great*, *drama group*, *noisy*, *full*, *boring*, *school lunches*).
- Ask students to read the text and to check the likes and dislikes that are similar to theirs.
- Let students compare their answers in pairs before you invite them to share their answers with the class.

Extra activity

Have students read the text again and try to remember all of Stella's likes and dislikes. Then divide the class into pairs and ask them to close their books and write down all the things they can remember. Set a time limit of two minutes, and then invite students to come to the board and add a like or a dislike. At the end of the activity, leave the list on the board as it may be useful for highlighting the plural forms and articles in the Study section of the lesson.

STUDY

2

- Refer students to the grammar table and explain that it focuses on singular and plural nouns. Ask students to find examples of nouns in the text in Exercise 1 and to say whether each noun is singular or plural. (See Teaching Tips, *English plural nouns*, page 25.)
- Have students complete the table with nouns. Remind them to refer back to the text, as most of the nouns appear there. Let them compare their answers in pairs before you check them as a class.
- Ask students to look at the completed table and elicit the spelling rules. You could also ask them to think of more examples for each spelling rule. Point out the difference in the pronunciation of the endings of words in the first and second groups. (See Teaching Tips, *The /ɪz/ sound*, page 28.)
- Refer students to the **Grammar Database** on page 52.

ANSWERS

boxes classes bus lunches cities people

3

- Ask students to complete the table with words from Exercise 1. You could ask more confident groups to cover the text and do this from memory.
- Let students compare their answers in pairs before you check them as a class.
- Point out that the words in italics in the explanations are articles (*a/an* and *the*) and elicit some of the rules for using articles; for example, *Do we use* a *or* an *before a vowel sound? Do we use* a, an, *or* the *for specific things?*
- Refer students to the **Grammar Database** on page 52.

ANSWERS

ice-cream hot school bus games

Extra activity

With monolingual groups, you might want to have students translate some of the sentences into their own language. This provides an opportunity for students to focus on form and to think about whether the same rules apply in their language. This is particularly useful in the case of articles where the rules can vary greatly between languages, and focusing on the differences may help students remember them.

PRACTICE

4

- Read the instruction aloud and go over the example.
- Have students do the exercise and let them check their answers in pairs before checking answers as a class.

ANSWERS

2 video 3 sandwich 4 woman

5

- Ask students to look at the words in the box and explain that they have to match them to the photos and write the number plus the appropriate plural noun.
- Focus students on the example and remind them to refer to the **Grammar Database** on page 52 for the spelling rules.
- Give students a couple of minutes to do the exercise and then let them compare their answers in pairs before you check them as a class.

Alternative procedure: less confident classes

Have students match the words to the pictures as a whole class.

ANSWERS

2 three glasses
3 two stories
4 two men
5 four apples
6 three sandwiches (clarify that they are club sandwiches)

6

- Refer students to the text and ask *What type of text is it?* (*a personal profile*) and *Where can you see a text like this?* (*a social networking site*).
- Ask students to read the text quickly and then to tell a partner three things about the person in the profile; for example, *He's from Washington. He likes cars. He plays basketball.*
- Set a time limit of three minutes for students to choose the correct options to complete the profile.
- Let students compare their answers in pairs and ask them to justify their answers by referring to the grammar rules; for example, *"Cars" has no article. It's a general thing and it's plural.*
- Call on students to share their answers with the class.

ANSWERS

2 a 3 - 4 a 5 - 6 an 7 a 8 the

7

- Have students look at the text and tell a partner which of the sentences are true for them. Tell them not to worry about the blanks at this stage.
- Draw students' attention to the example and then ask them to complete the rest of the sentences.
- Let students compare their answers in pairs before you check them as a class.

ANSWERS

2 the 3 a 4 the 5 an 6 -

WRITE AND SPEAK

8a

- Ask students to read the instructions and then model some possible sentences; for example, *I'm from London. My favorite color is blue*. To illustrate that some sentences are false, provide endings that are evidently false; for example, if you have brown eyes, say *I have blue eyes*.
- Set a time limit of two minutes for students to complete the sentences. Circulate and help students where necessary.

8b

- Call on a student to read the instructions aloud. Model the task by asking several students to read some of their sentences aloud and asking the class to decide if they're true or false.
- Divide the class into pairs and have students do the task.
- Invite students to tell the class what they found out about their partners.

Homework

Ask students to prepare a social networking page for themselves that includes a brief profile and lists of their likes and dislikes. Refer them to the texts in Exercises 1 and 6. Ask them to write about 50 words for each and to illustrate the page with photographs. If you're using an online platform with student profile pages, you could ask students to do this online, but make sure that you have parents' permission and that students are using a suitably secure platform. In the next class, have students compare their profiles and find likes and dislikes that are similar.

LISTENING AND VOCABULARY It's a small world!

Listen to a description of where things are from *Page 12*

STAGE	TIME	FOCUS
GET STARTED		Play a game to find out what countries students can name.
WORK WITH WORDS		Learn vocabulary for countries and the word endings used for nationalities. Talk about things that are famous in those countries.
SPEAK AND LISTEN		Listen and identify where things are from (listening subskill). Think about what you already know about the topic. Listen to someone talking about where his things are from.
REACT		Talk about where your things are from.

Get started

As the lesson focuses on countries and nationalities, find out what countries students know in English by playing *Alphabet Race* (see Games, page 33). For this game you can include *Z* and *Q* (Qatar) but omit *X*.

WORK WITH WORDS Countries and nationalities

1a 17

- Check that students know what countries and nationalities are and then have them look at the picture and elicit that it shows countries. Explain that a nationality describes the origin of the person or thing from a country and give an example (e.g., where you are from and your nationality). Highlight the plural form of each word (*country/countries, nationality/nationalities*).
- Divide the class into pairs. Ask students to match the pictures to the countries and to write the numbers in the chart.
- Play the track for students to check their answers. Stop the track after each answer and drill pronunciation. Get feedback from students to see how many they answered correctly. Highlight the word stress of each country. (See underlining in audio script below.)

ANSWERS / AUDIO SCRIPT 17

1 Italy 2 South Africa 3 Turkey 4 Japan 5 Brazil 6 Germany

1b 18

- Read the instructions aloud and go over the example with the class.
- Ask students to use the suffixes *-an*, *-ese*, *-ian*, *-n*, and *-ish* to complete the nationalities.
- Let students compare their answers in pairs before you play the track for them to check their answers.
- Continue the track for students to listen and repeat. You could also ask students to mark the stressed syllable in each word and then check answers as a class (see underlining in audio script below). Ask students to say when the word stress changes (*Italy/Italian, Japan/Japanese*).

ANSWERS / AUDIO SCRIPT 18

Brazil	*Brazilian*
Germany	German
Italy	Italian
Japan	Japanese
South Africa	South African
Turkey	Turkish

Extra activity

Have students draw two columns in their notebooks and write the countries and nationalities given in Exercise 1a. Divide the class into pairs and ask students to think of five more countries to add to their lists. Then ask them to write the nationality for each of the countries if they can. Set a time limit of three minutes. Circulate and help students by referring them to the suffixes in Exercise 1b. Have students compare their words in small groups and add any other countries and nationalities to their lists. Then ask students to share their ideas with the class and ask them what new countries they learned.

2

- Ask a student to read the instructions aloud and elicit some examples of countries and a famous place or thing for each one (e.g., *Italy/Pompeii, Japan/sushi*).
- Divide the class into pairs and have them think of something famous for each country. Set a time limit of three minutes. Circulate and help students with ideas.
- Stop the activity and invite students to come to the board and make a class list of ideas.

Extra activity

For extra practice, have students play *Memory* (see Games, page 29) with the countries from Exercise 1 and the things they are famous for. Prepare for this before class by cutting up 12 small squares of paper for each pair of students. Hand them out and ask students to write countries on six of the pieces of paper. On each of the remaining pieces, ask them to write the famous things. Before playing, ask students to say the words when they pick them up. Set a time limit of three minutes.

SPEAK AND LISTEN

3a

- Call on a student to read the instructions aloud. Then ask students to look at the pictures.
- Elicit a couple of ideas from the class for where the things are from. You could write the phrase *I think … is from …* on the board and ask students to use it in the activity.
- Divide the class into pairs and set a time limit of two minutes for the activity.
- Invite students to share their ideas with the class, but don't confirm them at this point.

3b ▶19

- Read the instructions aloud and refer students to the **Listening Tip**. Elicit that the topic for this activity is where the things in the pictures are from and recap some of the ideas from Exercise 3a. Point out that this is all they know about the topic so far.
- Play the track for students to check their ideas from Exercise 3a.
- Choose students to share the answers with the class.

ANSWERS / AUDIO SCRIPT ▶19

Jeans: Turkey T-shirt: Turkey Sunglasses: Italy
Oranges: South Africa Apples: Brazil Television: Japan
Phone: Japan

It's a small world!
You don't believe me? Look at my clothes.
I'm in the USA. These jeans ... are from Turkey. That's far away. And this T-shirt ... is Turkish too. These sunglasses are from Italy. A lot of the sunglasses in the world are Italian.
Let's look at some food now ... What about those oranges? They're from... South Africa. Wow, that's on the other side of the world! And where are these apples from? They're Brazilian. That's far away too.
What about all the technology? That television is from Japan. And ... my phone ... It's Japanese too.
Hi, Ricardo. ... That's my friend Ricardo. He's Colombian.
You see? It really *is* a small world!

4 ▶19

- Read the instructions aloud and give students a minute to read the sentences.
- Play the track for students to listen and choose the correct answers.
- Let students compare their answers in pairs before you check them as a class.

ANSWERS / AUDIO SCRIPT ▶19

2 B 3 A

See Exercise 3b for audio script.

Alternative procedure: less confident classes

Before checking the answers to Exercise 4, hand out the audio script. Then play the track and ask students to call out *stop* when it comes to each answer. When you've finished checking the answers, ask students to underline any new words or phrases and go through them as a class.

REACT

5

- Read the instructions aloud and give students a couple of minutes to think about some of their possessions and where they are from. Suggest that they think about their clothes, things they have at school, in their bedrooms, etc. Remind students that clothes often say where they were made on the label.
- Refer students to the PHRASE BYTES box and explain that these are some expressions they can use to talk about where their things are from. Model the phrases and have students repeat them.
- Divide the class into pairs and have students talk about where their things are from. Set a time limit of two minutes. You could also ask them to find similarities in their lists; for example, both have T-shirts from Vietnam.
- Monitor and note errors and good use of language to go over in a feedback session at the end of the activity. (See Teaching Tips, *Correcting errors effectively*, page 24.)
- Stop the activity and invite students to tell the class about where their things are from.

MOVE BEYOND

Ask students to do the Words & Beyond exercise on page 56.

Homework

Tell students that they are going to prepare a quiz about specific things and where they're from. Ask them to think of five things they have in their bedrooms and to find out where they're from. They should then write five multiple-choice statements about the things; for example:

A Samsung cell phone is from ...

A China B South Korea C Japan

Encourage students to make their quizzes as challenging as possible and not to use items with an obvious answer or choose things from only one country. Remind students to list only things that have a label indicating clearly where they're from. In the next class, divide the class into groups of four and have the students test each other.

GRAMMAR *This/that, these/those*

Talk about the things around you — *Page 13*

STAGE	TIME	FOCUS
GET STARTED		Play *Vocabulary Tennis* to review word categories from previous lessons.
READ AND LISTEN		Read and listen to a conversation at the market and label pictures.
STUDY		Read grammar explanations and complete examples with *this/that, these/those*.
PRACTICE		Practice using *this/that, these/those* in controlled exercises.
SPEAK		Talk to a partner about your things and practice using the target language.

Get started

To review vocabulary from previous lessons and find out what students know about the vocabulary areas in this lesson, play a game of *Vocabulary Tennis* (see Games, page 29). Include the categories *colors*, *international words*, *countries*, *fruit*, and *clothes* (the last two categories being those that appear in this lesson). You might want to make a note of any new vocabulary on the board and check that students know what the words mean at the end of the game.

READ AND LISTEN Grammar in context

1 ▶20

- Read the instructions aloud and ask students to look at the picture and say what they think the fruits are. The objective of this stage is to find out what students know, but don't confirm any answers until they've read and listened to the text.
- Play the track for students to read and listen to the conversation and write the names of the fruits.
- Let students compare their answers in pairs before you check them as a class. When checking answers, ask students *What's at the front/back?* (This will help make the language point clearer in Exercise 2.)

ANSWERS / AUDIO SCRIPT ▶20

At the front: apples, watermelon
At the back: *bananas*, grapes, fruit salad

See Student's Book, page 15, for audio script.

STUDY

2

- Read the instructions aloud and check that students understand *here* and *there*.
- Have students complete the table with *this*, *that*, *these*, and *those*.
- Let students compare their answers in pairs before you check them as a class.
- Refer students to the **Grammar Database** on page 52.

ANSWERS

that These

Extra activity

Ask students to practice reading the conversation in Exercise 1 in pairs. Encourage them to act out the conversation and to point out the things they're talking about, especially when they're using *this/that, these/those*. In order to get students to practice the conversation from memory, you could do this activity as a disappearing conversation (See Teaching Tips, *Disappearing conversation*, page 26).

PRACTICE

3

- Ask the class to look at the picture. Point out that it's a market stall (you might have to elicit or explain the difference between *store* and *stall*) and ask them to say what they can see at the front and back of the stall.
- Ask students to complete the sentences with *this*, *that*, *these*, and *those*.
- Let students compare their answers in pairs before you check them as a class.

ANSWERS

2 This 3 these 4 that 5 Those 6 this

4

- Point out that this is another market stall and ask students to say what they can see.
- Ask students to read the conversation silently to check their ideas. Tell them not to worry about the blanks.
- Ask students to complete the conversation with *this*, *that*, *these*, and *those*.
- Call on different students to give the answers.

ANSWERS

2 that 3 this 4 these 5 this

SPEAK

5

- Ask a student to read the instructions aloud and model the task by putting some of your things on the desk (e.g., keys, cell phone, pens, lunchbox, purse/wallet).
- Refer students to the useful phrases and invite different students to come to the desk and ask you questions about your things. Encourage students to ask extra questions using the expressions from the PHRASE BYTES box on page 12; for example, *Where's it from? What's on the label?*
- Divide the class into pairs and set a time limit of three minutes for students to do the task using things from their bags or pockets.

Extra activity

Ask students to draw their own market stall with some things at the front and some at the back. You could suggest that they include things from the unit. Divide the class into pairs and have them ask and answer questions using *this/that, these/those*; for example, *What are those?* At the end of the task, have the pair sit with another pair. Ask them to show the other pair their partner's picture and say what the things are; for example, *That's a bicycle and these are comic books.* Ask the groups to decide which market stall has the most interesting things.

Homework

Ask students to imagine that they're at a market in an unusual place. To generate ideas, show pictures of unusual markets around the world (e.g., a Mexican street market, a floating market in Thailand, a flea market in Paris, a food market in China). Ask students to write a short conversation (about 50 words) taking place in one of these markets, using the conversations in Exercises 1 and 4 to help them. Ask them to include *this/that, these/those*. In the next class, have students read each other's conversations and try to guess where the market is. If there's time, students could act out their conversations in pairs. Monitor and note good use of language and errors for feedback at the end of the task.

LANGUAGE & BEYOND SCHOOL SKILLS

Be a good classmate

Page 14

STAGE	TIME	FOCUS
GET STARTED		Review classroom language and use it to write conversations in the classroom.
SPEAK AND READ		Match expressions to describe classroom behavior to pictures and talk about how often you do those things.
DO		Decide whether classroom behavior is good or bad and justify your ideas.
REFLECT		Talk about the importance of being a good classmate.
EXTEND		Discuss good and bad behavior in other situations outside school.

SCHOOL SKILLS

BE A GOOD CLASSMATE
It is a good idea to establish what's expected of students early on in the course, but just "laying down the law" may not be the best way to encourage good behavior. Students will probably be more motivated if they have the opportunity to think about and discuss what constitutes good behavior and why it's important. This also moves the focus away from the individual student and toward the group as a whole. This lesson asks students to think about what type of behavior is best for learning, and it can be used as a foundation for encouraging good behavior throughout the course.

Get started

The lesson is concerned with the skill of being a good classmate, so it's useful for students to review and practice some classroom language. Write the following jumbled questions on the board:

- *repeat / that / you / please? / Can* (*Can you repeat that, please?*)
- *What's / our language? / "bus" / in* (*What's "bus" in our language?*)
- *go / the restroom / to / Can / I / please?* (*Can I go to the restroom, please?*)
- *help / Can / me? / you* (*Can you help me?*)
- *spell / "category" / you / Can / please?* (*Can you spell "category," please?*)

Ask students to work in pairs and put the words in order to make questions. When you check answers, check that they understand all the questions. Ask what word we use to be polite (*please*). Then ask students to write short conversations with some of the questions. Monitor and note errors and good use of language to go over in a feedback session at the end of the activity.

SPEAK AND READ

1a

- Ask students to describe what they can see in the picture.
- Go over the instructions and the descriptions in the box.
- Divide the class into pairs and have them match the situations to the descriptions.
- Invite different students to give their answers and check that students understand all the vocabulary.

ANSWERS
1 b 2 d 3 c 4 e 5 a

1b

- Go over the instructions and explain the meanings of the frequency adverbs if necessary. Elicit answers to the question.
- Ask students to write the frequency adverbs next to the phrases in the box according to their own class behavior. Invite students to share their answers with the class.

DO

2a

- Go over the instructions and elicit an example; for example, *It's good to listen to the teacher in class.*
- Divide the class into pairs and have them classify the descriptions and add more things if possible.
- Invite students to share their answers with the class. You could ask whether any answers can be both good and bad (e.g., *be quiet*).

SUGGESTED ANSWERS

It's good to … in class.	It's bad to … in class.
help classmates	be noisy
be quiet and listen to the teacher	use a phone
throw trash in the wastebasket	

2b

- Read the instructions aloud and refer students to the sentence stems and the phrases in Exercise 1.
- Divide the class into pairs and set a time limit of three minutes for students to complete the sentences. Tell students to try to think of more reasons of their own.
- Invite students to share their answers with the class. Elicit further reasons for each point.

ANSWERS
1 quiet 2 noisy 3 help classmates
4 throw trash in the wastebasket

REFLECT

3

- Read the instructions and the questions aloud. Then divide the class into small groups for students to discuss the questions.
- Refer students to the useful expressions in the PHRASE BYTES box and set a time limit of two minutes for the task.

- Stop the activity and invite students to share their answers with the class.
- Call on a student to read the REFLECTION POINT aloud. Then ask the class whether they agree or disagree, encouraging them to give reasons.

EXTEND

4

- Read the instructions aloud and explain that students have to choose just one of the situations and that they should think of reasons to justify their ideas.
- Refer students to the PHRASE BYTES box and encourage them to use these and the structures from Exercise 2b to justify their answers.
- Divide the class into small groups and set a time limit of three minutes for the task.
- When students have finished, invite them to share their ideas with the class and ask other students if they agree or disagree.

Homework

Ask students to create a poster for one of the situations they've talked about in the lesson (at school, with friends, or at home). Explain that they should include two things that are good to do and two things that are bad to do and their reasons, and encourage them to illustrate their posters. In the next class, have students display their posters around the classroom and ask them to circulate and decide which posters they like best.

SPEAKING Is it new?

Describe things

Page 15

STAGE	TIME	FOCUS
GET STARTED		Review *this/that, these/those*.
SPEAK		Match adjectives to their opposites.
LISTEN		Listen to conversations and identify the things the people are describing. Complete the conversations and practice phrases for describing things (speaking subskill).
ACT		Write a conversation describing things, and act it out for other students.

Get started

Review *this/that, these/those*. Prepare pictures of things students know the words for (food, clothes, electronics, etc.), making sure some pictures show one item and others show a number of items. Give some students a picture and place others around the classroom. Invite students to either hold up a picture if they have one, or point to a picture, and to say something about it using *this*, *that*, *these*, or *those*.

SPEAK

1

- Choose a student to read the instructions aloud.
- Divide the class into pairs and have students match the adjectives to their opposites.
- Call on students to share their answers with the class. As students give the answers, take the opportunity to drill pronunciation.

ANSWERS

1 c 2 a 3 d 4 b

Extra activity

Ask students to work in pairs to think of more adjectives and their opposites (e.g., *young/old*, *happy/sad*). Set a time limit of two minutes for students to think of as many adjective pairs as they can. Circulate and help generate ideas. Then have students work with another pair and compare their lists, adding any new adjective pairs that they learn. Ask pairs to share some of their examples with the class. Encourage students to keep a list of adjectives with their opposites in their notebooks and to add to them as they learn new words.

LISTEN

2 21

- Ask the class to look at the pictures and say what they can see.
- Call on a student to read the instructions aloud, and then ask students to cover the texts.
- Play the track for students to listen and decide what things the people describe.
- Ask students to read the conversations to check their answers and let them compare their answers in pairs.
- Call on students to share their answers with the class.

ANSWERS / AUDIO SCRIPT 21

Conversation 1: a backpack
Conversation 2: sunglasses
Conversation 3: a house (and its neighbors) and a room

1
Becca: I can't find my backpack.
Kent: What color is it?
Becca: It's red, and it's really old.
Kent: Is that it on the chair?
Becca: Yes, that's it.

2
Anita: Do you like Vicky's sunglasses? They're new.
Zac: They're very nice.
Vicky: Thanks. They're Italian.

3
Zac: What's your house like?
Lily: It's OK, but the neighbors are really noisy.
Zac: What about your room? Is it big?
Lily: No, my room's very small.

3 ▶21

- Ask a student to read the instructions aloud and refer students to the adjectives in Exercise 1.
- Have students complete the conversations, and then allow them to compare their answers in pairs.
- Play the track again for students to listen and check their answers.
- Call on students to share their answers with the class.

ANSWERS / AUDIO SCRIPT ▶21

See underlining in audio script in Exercise 2.

4 ▶22

- Play the track for students to listen and repeat the sentences.
- Encourage them to copy the intonation of the speakers and to use gestures if they like.

AUDIO SCRIPT ▶22

1 What color is it?
2 It's red, and it's really old.
3 They're very nice.
4 What's your house like?
5 The neighbors are really noisy.
6 My room's very small.

Extra activity

Divide the class into pairs and ask students to practice the conversations. Give them two or three minutes to practice, and then invite pairs to act out one of the conversations for the class.

ACT

5 ▶23

- Read the instructions aloud and check that students understand the task by asking them to suggest some things they could include for each of the conversations.
- Refer students to the PHRASEBOOK and play the track for them to listen and repeat the phrases. Check that students understand the questions by eliciting some possible answers; for example, *What's it like? It's big.*
- Divide the class into pairs and set a time limit of 10 minutes for them to write and practice their conversations. Remind students to use the phrases from the PHRASEBOOK in the conversation.
- Monitor and note errors and good use of language to go over in a feedback session at the end of the activity.
- After five minutes, have students present their conversations to the class.
- At the end of the activity, ask the group to decide which conversations were the best.

Alternative procedure: less confident classes

Less confident students may feel uncomfortable presenting their conversations in front of the whole class, in which case, you can divide the class into groups of four and have the pairs present their conversations to each other.

Homework

Ask students to write two conversations similar to the ones in Exercise 2. As in Exercise 5, ask them to write about different things and to use different adjectives. Remind them to refer to the useful expressions in the PHRASEBOOK and to write 20–30 words for each conversation. In the next class, divide the class into pairs and have them compare their conversations and say what things are different.

In the next class, students will write about their things, and it is suggested that they use photos. Ask students to bring in photos of three things that are important to them (e.g., a pet, a game, a musical instrument).

WRITING My things

Write a description of a thing Page 16

STAGE	TIME	FOCUS
GET STARTED		Play a guessing game to review adjectives.
SPEAK AND READ		Describe pictures, read descriptions of the pictures, and learn how to use adjectives (writing subskill).
PRACTICE		Focus on word order in sentences with adjectives.
DISCUSS		Talk about a thing you have at school to help you plan a description.
WRITE		Follow instructions to write descriptions of three things.
SHARE		Read your description to your classmates. Choose your favorite description.

Get started

As the lesson focuses on using adjectives in written descriptions, review the adjectives that students have encountered in previous lessons (e.g., *big*, *yellow*, *nice*), and prepare a list in advance. Remind students that adjectives are words that describe nouns (things, places, or people). Explain that you're going to call out adjectives and they have to think of one thing they associate with each adjective (e.g., *big – brother*, *yellow – banana*). Ask them to write their words individually in random order, not in a list. When you've read all the adjectives, divide students into pairs and have them read their words to their partners, who should guess what the adjective was for each word; for example:

A: *Banana*
B: *Yellow?*
A: *That's right. A banana is yellow.*

SPEAK AND READ

1a

- Tell students that they are going to look at things that are important to somebody. Ask them to look at the pictures and say what those things are (*a bike, two elephants, a T-shirt*).
- Read the instructions aloud and ask students not to read the texts for the moment. Remind them that adjectives are used to describe nouns and elicit some phrases to describe the photos (e.g., *a small elephant, a blue bike*).
- Divide the class into pairs and set a time limit of two minutes for students to do the task. Remind them to write down their ideas.
- Stop the activity and invite several students to come to the board one at a time and write their ideas.

1b

- Ask a student to read the instructions aloud and refer students to the list of adjectives they've written on the board.
- Have students read the descriptions to see if they use the same adjectives as the ones on the board.

> **Alternative procedure: less confident classes**
> With less confident classes, have students read the texts one by one and check the adjectives used as a class after each text.

2

- Refer the class to the HOW TO box and call on students to read each of the points.
- As word order can sometimes be a problem, ask students *Do adjectives go before or after the verb* be? (*after*), and point out that this is regardless of the position of the noun in the sentence; for example, *This is a great photo / This photo is great.* Remind students that *am/are/is* can be negative; for example, *It isn't expensive*. Elicit some examples from the class to check understanding. Have students underline the other adjectives in the picture descriptions and compare their work in pairs. Ask students to match the adjectives with the rules.
- Call on students to share their answers with the class.

ANSWERS

new cool fast favorite great African local big

PRACTICE

3

- Read the instructions aloud and elicit the first sentence.
- Have students put the words in order to make the remaining sentences.
- Let students compare their answers in pairs before you check them as a class.
- Ask students which of the sentences in Exercise 3 have plural nouns (*2, 3, 5*) and whether the adjective changes form for singular or plural nouns (*It doesn't*).

ANSWERS

1 This is my new phone.
2 These sunglasses are really nice. / These are really nice sunglasses.
3 This is my collection of Japanese comics.
4 My computer isn't very fast.
5 My favorite jeans are really old.

> **Fast finishers**
> Ask fast finishers to rewrite the sentences in Exercise 3 by changing the last word in each sentence; for example, *This is my new hat; These sunglasses are really old.*

DISCUSS

4

- Go over the instructions and explain that students are going to describe one thing they have at school. This will help them prepare to write descriptions in the next exercise. Divide the class into pairs.
- If students have brought photos, ask them to think about how they will describe the thing in one of their photos. If they haven't, have them draw a picture of the thing they are going to describe.
- Set a time limit of four minutes for pairs to describe their possessions to each other. Monitor and note errors and good use of language to go over in a feedback session at the end of the activity.

WRITE

5

- Explain that students are now going to write descriptions of three of their possessions. Ask them to write about 20 words for each description and to use ideas from their discussion in Exercise 4.
- Go over the three steps for writing. Refer them back to the HOW TO box to help them. Set a time limit of 10 minutes for writing and circulate and help as necessary.
- When students have finished writing, ask them to check their descriptions against the points in Exercise 5 to make sure they have followed all the steps.

SHARE

6

- Ask students to read their descriptions aloud to the class. If you have a large class, you could have students do this in groups.
- When students have finished reading their descriptions, invite them to say which picture and description they liked the best.

> **Homework**
> Ask students to write six sentences about their things, four true and two false, using different adjectives; for example, *My dog is really old.* Encourage them to find or draw pictures to illustrate their sentences. Refer students to the HOW TO box and encourage them to write complete sentences and to use *really/very*. In the next class, divide the class into small groups and have students show each other their pictures and read their sentences aloud for the group to decide whether they are true or false.

VOCABULARY Things

1

- Have students look at the website and explain that they have to label the icons with the words. Point out that at least one letter of each word is given.
- Ask students to complete the words.
- Let students compare their answers in pairs before you check them as a class.

ANSWERS
1 sandwich 2 T-shirt 3 ice cream 4 soccer ball
5 backpack 6 bike 7 phone 8 game console

Countries and nationalities

2

- Read the instructions aloud and point out that the first few letters of each word are given.
- Ask students to complete the words for countries and nationalities.
- Let students compare their answers in pairs before you check them as a class.

ANSWERS
1 Brazilian; Brazil
2 Italy; Italian
3 South African; South Africa
4 Turkey; Turkish
5 Japanese; Japan
6 Germany; German

GRAMMAR Plural nouns; *a/an, the*

3

- Go over the instructions. Point out that students may need to indicate no article (-) or change words in parentheses into the plural form.
- Ask students to read through the text first without worrying about the blanks.
- Ask students to complete the message with *a*, *an*, *the*, -, or the plural of the noun in parentheses.
- Let students compare their answers in pairs before you check them as a class.

ANSWERS
1 a 2 cities 3 an 4 – 5 The 6 classes
7 the 8 a 9 videos

This/that, these/those

4

- Ask students to look at the picture and say what they can see; for example, *Those are sunglasses.*
- Explain that this is a description someone has written for a social networking site. Encourage students to read through the text first to help them understand.
- Ask students to complete the description with *this*, *that*, *these*, and *those*.
- Let students compare their answers in pairs before you check them as a class.

ANSWERS
1 This 2 These 3 This 4 Those 5 That 6 that

SKILLS CHECK

- Ask students to think about what they've learned in this unit and to check the sentences.
- Divide the class into pairs to discuss what they've learned, and use this as an opportunity to review anything students still have difficulties with.

Extra Resources

Go to the Teacher's Resource Center at mee2.macmillaneducation.com for:

- downloadable audio and audio scripts for the Student's Book and Workbook
- videos, video worksheets, and video scripts
- extra vocabulary at two levels of difficulty
- extra grammar at two levels of difficulty
- culture lessons, with full teacher's notes
- school skills lessons, with full teacher's notes
- Speaking Database materials
- the *Move Beyond Intro A Level* wordlist
- downloadable PDF and Word tests for Unit 1 (all skills)
- tips for using the Grammar Database
- extra reading materials
- and more!

Go to the Workbook pages 70–81 for further practice material.

2 UNIT PEOPLE

IN THE PICTURE Family and friends

Talk about your family and friends *Pages 18–19*

STAGE	TIME	FOCUS
GET STARTED		Play a matching game to review family words.
WORK WITH WORDS		Review adjectives and their opposites. Learn and practice using family words. Practice the pronunciation of the /æ/ sound. Watch a video about someone's family and friends.
SPEAK		Talk about your family.

Get started

In order to find out what family words students know, prepare a number of pictures showing famous pairs; for example, George Bush Sr. and Jr. (father and son), Ben and Casey Affleck (brothers), Ashley and Mary-Kate Olsen (sisters), Brad Pitt and Angelina Jolie (husband and wife). The pairs should not be in the same picture. Try to choose pairs that you think students will recognize. Post the pictures randomly around the classroom. Divide the class into pairs and tell them that they have three minutes to walk around and decide which famous people go together and what the relationships are. Model an example to make sure students understand the task. After three minutes, stop the activity and ask students how many pairs they have. Invite them to share their answers with the class and write the people and the family words on the board.

WORK WITH WORDS Family

1 RECALL

- Ask a student to read the instructions aloud and elicit an example that isn't in the exercise (e.g., *cold – hot*).
- Divide the class into pairs and set a time limit of one minute for students to write the opposites.
- Call on students to share their answers with the class.
- Ask students to do the Work with Words task on page 57.

ANSWERS
1 different 2 terrible 3 big 4 good 5 noisy 6 new

Alternative procedure: less confident classes
Write the opposite adjectives on the board in a random order. Ask students to match the opposites on the board to the adjectives in Exercise 1.

2a

- Ask a student to read the instructions aloud and refer students to the PHRASE BYTES box. Explain that the phrases are useful for the task and give some examples; for example, *I think the girl in picture 9 is Leo's sister.*
- Divide the class into pairs and set a time limit of two minutes for them to look at the pictures and guess whether they are Leo's friends or family members.
- Don't check the answers at this stage, as students will listen and check their answers in Exercise 2b.

ANSWERS
Friends: photos 1, 4, and 6
Family: photos 2, 3, 5, 7, and 9

2b ▶24

- Ask students to listen and check their ideas from Exercise 2a and to match the names in the box to the pictures.
- Play the track once or twice for students to do the tasks.
- Ask students to compare their answers in pairs and to give reasons if they can; for example, *That's Dan. He has a red T-shirt.*
- Invite students to share their answers with the class.

ANSWERS / AUDIO SCRIPT ▶24
Carlos – 4 Dan – 1 Emma – 6

Jamie: Who are all those people on your phone?
Leo: This is my friend Dan in the red T-shirt. He's my best friend. ... That's my little brother, Tom. He's nine, and he's very noisy. ... And this is my grandma and grandpa. They're very old.
Jamie: Who's that?
Leo: Oh, that's my friend Carlos with his mother and father. His mother's Mexican. Carlos is an only child, so he doesn't have brothers and sisters. ... This is my dad here in the horrible jacket! And this is my friend Emma. She's with her grandmother and grandfather. She's their favorite grandchild!
Jamie: Is that your mom there?
Leo: Yes, that's my mom. She's fantastic. This person doesn't have a picture, but I think it's my teacher, Ms. Carter.
Jamie: And who's that?
Leo: That's my big sister, Ella. She's 14.

3a ▶24

- Go over the instructions and call on students to read the family words aloud. Elicit the meaning of *an only child* (*someone who has no brothers or sisters*). Point out that some of the words have the same meaning (e.g., *grandfather-grandpa*), but they are used in reference to different pictures, so students will have to listen carefully to catch the specific word or words used to describe each picture.
- Play the track again for students to match the family words to the pictures. Since students have to find the word or words in the box that match each picture, it is a good idea to pause the recording after the description of each picture to give students time to find the relevant words and write the number of the picture.
- Let students compare their answers in pairs, but don't check them at this stage.

AUDIO SCRIPT ▶24

See Exercise 2b for audio script.

3b ▶25

- Play the track for students to listen and check their answers from Exercise 3a.
- Call on students to share their answers with the class.

ANSWERS / AUDIO SCRIPT ▶25

brother – 2　dad – 5　father – 4　grandchild – 6
grandfather – 6　grandma – 3　grandmother – 6　grandpa – 3
mom – 7　mother – 4　only child – 4　sister – 9

4a ▶26 PRONOUNCE

- Read the instructions aloud and model the /æ/ sound. Ask students to imitate the sound you make.
- Play the track for students to listen and repeat.

AUDIO SCRIPT ▶26

See Student's Book, page 20, for audio script.

4b ▶27

- Read the instructions aloud and have students look at the words.
- Play the track for students to listen and repeat.

AUDIO SCRIPT ▶27

See Student's Book, page 20, for audio script.

5

- Go over the instructions and the example. Model the task by calling on different students and asking them questions; for example, *Who's in picture 4? That's Carlos and his mother and father.*
- Divide the class into pairs and set a time limit of two minutes for the activity.

6 THE MOVING PICTURE ▶

- Call on a student to read the instructions aloud.
- Play the video for students to watch and find the answers to the questions.

ANSWERS / VIDEO SCRIPT

Grandpa – family　Brother – family　Grandma – family
Rosie (sister) – family　Mom – family
Mrs. Peters – friend　Three friends

Dan: Hello, Grandpa. What are you doing?
Grandpa: I'm working. I'll see you tomorrow.

Brother: Hi.
Dan: Hi, big brother.
Brother: How's it going?
Dan: I'm good, thanks. I'll see you later.

Dan: Hi, Grandma.
Grandma: Hi, Dan.
Dan: I'll see you tomorrow.
Grandma: OK. Good.

Dan: Hi, Rosie.
Dan: Ugh – sisters!

Dan: Hi, Mom.
Mom: Hi, Dan. I'll see you at home!

Dan: Hello, Mrs. Peters.
Mrs. Peters: Hello, Dan.

Dan: Hi, guys.
Friend 1: Hi.
Friend 2: Hi, Dan.
Friend 3: Hi, Dan.

SPEAK

7

- This task would work well with students bringing in photos of their families. If you would like to do this, ask students in the previous class to bring photos to the next class. Where students have cell phones and are allowed to use them at school, you could ask them to take photos of their family on their phones to show in class.
- Read the instructions aloud and give students five minutes to draw their pictures if they don't have photos. If they have photos, ask them to think about who each person is and to think of something else to say about each one; for example, *This is my grandma. She's 80!*
- Refer students to the PHRASE BYTES box. Model the expressions and have students repeat them.
- Divide the class into pairs and have students show each other their pictures or photos and talk about their families. Set a time limit of three minutes.
- Monitor and note good use of language and errors for feedback at the end of the task.
- Invite students to tell the class something about their partner's family. Then give feedback and error correction.

MOVE BEYOND

Ask students to do the Words & Beyond exercise on page 57.

Homework

Ask students to use their pictures from Exercise 7 and write a short description (60 words) of their family for a blog. Remind them to use the expressions from the PHRASE BYTES box and to include some extra information about the people. If students have a school blog page, you could ask them to add the description and pictures or photos to the page. In the next class, have students work in small groups and read each other's descriptions. Ask them to find things they have in common (e.g., *We both have two brothers*; *Our moms are young*) and share them with the class.

READING I have a new phone

Read text messages

Page 20

STAGE	TIME	FOCUS
GET STARTED		Review language from previous lessons in a game of *Broken Telephone*.
SPEAK AND READ		Talk about people in your telephone contact list. Identify the text type to help you understand a text (reading subskill). Read and understand instant messages. Learn new words related to cell phones.
REACT		Talk about when you use your phone and what for. Write a text message.

MOVE BEYOND FOR TEACHERS

Text messages

Text messages, also known as SMS, are short written messages usually sent between cell phones. It's a service that is widely used across the world and has transformed the way people communicate. In order to communicate the message more effectively and concisely, people use abbreviations and "emoticons" (e.g., ☺, ☹). Instant messaging is a similar form of communication and is also extremely popular, especially with younger people. It's motivating for students to work on text messages in class, and due to their brevity, they can be used with all levels. If phones are permitted in the classroom, you can even have students use their phones to send each other real text messages in English.

Get started

Students look at text messages in the lesson, so you could lead in by preteaching *message* and playing a game of *Broken Telephone* (see Games, page 29) in which students have to pass on messages. Prepare sentences that recycle language from previous lessons; for example, *I like a big watermelon on a hot day. The Japanese children are in South Africa.* At the end of the activity have students reflect on the topic of messages by asking the whole class *Is this a good way to send messages? How do you send messages?*

SPEAK AND READ

1

- Read the instructions aloud. Then give some examples of people in your contact list and tell students about them; for example, *Julia is my sister.*
- Refer students to the PHRASE BYTES box and ask them if you used any of the useful expressions.
- Give students a couple of minutes to write the names. Then divide the class into pairs and set a time limit of three minutes for the task.
- Invite different students to tell the class about their contact lists. At the end of the activity, give feedback on good use of language and errors.

2 28

- Ask students to look at the pictures, read the first sentence of each message, and guess the answers to the questions. Don't confirm answers at this point.
- Point out that these are text messages and the pictures are of the people sending the messages.
- Ask a student to read the instructions aloud and refer students to the **Reading Tip**.
- Ask students to read the messages and answer the questions. Don't play the audio at this point. It is an extra feature, and a suggestion for using it in class is included at the end of the lesson.
- Let students compare their answers in pairs before you check them as a class.

ANSWERS

The messages are all from Leo.
They're for Emma, Dan, and Carlos.

3

- Read the instructions aloud and set a time limit of three minutes for the task. Tell students not to worry about understanding everything at this stage but to underline any new words for discussion at the end of the task.
- Stop the activity and ask students to compare their answers in pairs. Tell them to point to the part of the text where the answer is.
- When students have compared their answers, invite them to share their answers with the class and discuss any new words they've underlined.

ANSWERS

1 Leo and Dan 2 Leo 3 Leo 4 Emma
5 Leo and Dan 6 Ms. Carter

Fast finishers

Ask fast finishers to write another message for each conversation.

4

- Read the instructions aloud and refer students to the example. Point out that some letters of the words are given.
- Ask students to complete the words using the messages in Exercise 2 to help them.
- Let students compare their answers in pairs before you check them as a class.

ANSWERS

2 photo 3 games 4 internet 5 text messages

REACT

5

- Read the instructions and the questions aloud. Then refer students to the useful phrases in the PHRASE BYTES box. Elicit some possible endings for the phrases.
- Give students a minute to think about their answers. Then divide the class into pairs to ask and answer the questions. Encourage students to extend their answers; for example, *My best friend uses her phone to take photos. She loves the camera!*
- Invite students to share their answers and take a quick survey to find out what they use their phones for.

MOVE BEYOND

Call on a student to read the instructions aloud.

Ask students to look at the people on pages 18–19 and think about what Leo wants to say to them.

Set a time limit of three minutes for students to write their messages. Circulate and help where necessary, both with ideas and language.

Divide the class into pairs and have students trade messages. Ask them to read each other's messages and match them to the people on pages 18–19.

Invite students to read their messages aloud to the class.

Recorded reading text 28

As the written messages could just as easily be spoken, they provide a nice model for speaking and pronunciation practice. Have students read the messages between Leo and Emma again and then practice reading both parts aloud. Monitor and help students with pronunciation. Then ask students to just listen and read the messages in the first conversation as you play the track. Finally, explain that you are going to play the track again and that students should read the conversation along with the recording. Ask them to use their voices in the same way, focusing on intonation. Repeat the activity with the remaining conversations.

Homework

Ask students to think of three people to "send" text messages to (e.g., family members or friends), and to write short text messages to each of them (10–15 words for each). In the next class, divide the class into small groups and have students read their text messages aloud for their group to guess who the message is for.

GRAMMAR *Have*

Talk about your things, ideas, and problems *Page 21*

STAGE	TIME	FOCUS
GET STARTED		Review text messages from the previous lesson and focus on the meaning and form of *have*.
READ AND LISTEN		Read and listen to a conversation about choosing a present for someone.
STUDY		Complete examples with correct forms of *have*.
PRACTICE		Practice using *have* in controlled exercises. Use *have* to write a survey.
SPEAK		Do a survey to find out more about a classmate.

Get started

In order to review the text messages from the previous lesson and focus on examples of *have*, write the following sentences on the board:-

I have a new p ________ . (Leo)
You have the wrong n ________ . (Ms. Carter)
Does it have the i ________ *on it?* (Dan)
We have a lot of h ________ . (Dan)
We don't have t ________ *for games today.* (Dan)

Divide the class into small groups and explain that the sentences are from the text messages on page 20. Ask students to remember the word that goes in each blank and who said it. Check answers as a class and explain to students that we use *have* to talk about real and abstract possession; for example, *I have a laptop*; *You have the wrong number*.

READ AND LISTEN Grammar in context

1 29

- Ask students to look at the picture and elicit who's talking (*two friends*).
- Read the instructions aloud and play the track for students to read and listen to the conversation.
- Give students a minute to complete the sentences.
- Let students compare their answers in pairs before you check them as a class. You could also ask students to suggest a present for Clara's dad.

ANSWERS / AUDIO SCRIPT 29

birthday present

See Student's Book, page 23, for audio script.

STUDY

2

- Read the instructions aloud and refer students to the grammar table. Point out that it focuses on *have*. Explain that we use *have* with things, family, ideas, problems, etc.
- Ask students to find examples of *have* in the conversation and then to complete the table.
- Let students compare their answers in pairs before you check them as a class.
- Ask students to look at the completed table and point out the contractions *don't* and *doesn't*. Elicit the full form of the verbs in each case, but explain that we normally use contractions in the negative form.
- Refer students to the **Grammar Database** on page 53.

ANSWERS

Have (I, you, we, they)	
✓ Affirmative	✗ Negative
I have a problem.	*I don't have a present.*
Questions	Short answers
Do you have an idea?	*No, I don't.*

Has (he, she, it)	
✓ Affirmative	✗ Negative
He has a laptop.	*He doesn't have a tablet.*
Questions	Short answers
Does he have a tablet?	*Yes, he does.*

PRACTICE

3

- Explain that in this exercise Clara talks about her house and what it has in it.
- Read the instructions aloud and go over the example. Suggest that students read through the text briefly before trying to complete the sentences.
- Ask students to complete the sentences with *have* or *don't have*.
- Let students compare their answers in pairs before you check them as a class.

ANSWERS

2 don't have 3 have 4 have 5 have 6 don't have

4

- Explain that in this exercise, Albert talks about his family and things he has.
- Read the instructions aloud and ask students to look at the pictures and the example. Remind students to use affirmative and negative sentences.
- Set a time limit of three minutes for students to write their sentences.
- Let students check their answers in pairs before you check them as a class.

ANSWERS

2 He doesn't have a brother.
3 He has a laptop.
4 He doesn't have a tablet.
5 He doesn't have internet.
6 He has a lot of/some books.

Fast finishers

Ask fast finishers to rewrite the sentences in Exercise 4 so they're true for them.

5 ▶30

- Explain that in this exercise, Clara talks to a friend about her favorite movie.
- Read the instructions aloud and refer students to the example. Point out that they will use different forms of *have* and remind them to refer to the tables in Exercise 2 for help.
- Ask students to complete the conversation.
- Let students compare their answers in pairs.
- Play the track for students to check their answers. Then call on students to share their answers with the class. With less confident groups, you might want to stop the track for each answer and replay it if necessary.

ANSWERS / AUDIO SCRIPT ▶30

2 don't 3 do 4 Does 5 doesn't 6 Do
7 do

See Student's Book, page 21, for audio script.

6

- Ask students to look at the survey questions and then to write three more questions to ask a partner using *have*.
- Circulate and help students where necessary.

SPEAK

7

- Divide the class into pairs and set a time limit of three minutes.
- Ask students to ask and answer the questions in the survey in Exercise 6 and the questions they wrote. Encourage them to extend their answers; for example, *Do you have a TV in your room? Yes, I do. It's old, but it's really big!*
- Monitor and make notes of good use of language and errors for feedback at the end of the task.
- Invite students to tell the class something about their partners. Then give feedback on good language and errors.

Alternative procedure: more confident classes

Rather than doing the survey in pairs, you could do a whole class survey. Have students prepare their questions in pairs and write them on a piece of paper. Collect all the pieces of paper and choose one question from each pair and write it on the board. (You could use more questions if it's a small class). Have students copy the questions in their notebooks and give them five minutes to talk to as many people as possible and to put a check if a person says yes. Then stop the activity and call on students to share some of their results with the class.

Homework: less confident classes

Ask students to use their partners' answers from the survey in Exercises 6 and 7 to write a brief description (50–60 words) of what the person has. Refer them to the text in Exercise 3 and suggest that they write a similar text, but point out that they'll need to use the third person singular form (*has*). In the next class, have students display their texts around the classroom. Then ask them to walk around and read the descriptions to guess who the people are.

Homework: more confident classes

If you followed the alternative procedure, ask students to use their classmates' answers from the survey to write a brief description (50–60 words) of what they have. If not, ask them to interview a friend or family member outside of school. Refer them to the text in Exercise 3 and suggest that they write a similar text. In the next class, discuss what most students have and don't have, and anything unusual that people have.

LISTENING AND VOCABULARY Whose is it?

Listen to a quiz show Page 22

STAGE	TIME	FOCUS
GET STARTED		Play *Find Someone Who …* to review *have*.
WORK WITH WORDS		Learn vocabulary for parts of the body. Practice using the vocabulary by listening to descriptions and drawing pictures (listening subskill).
SPEAK AND LISTEN		Answer quiz questions and listen to a quiz.
REACT		Talk about the quiz and parts of the body.

Get started

Play *Find Someone Who …* (see Games, page 33) to review and practice *have*. You could use any information about students that came up in the survey in Exercises 6 and 7 on page 22 or the related homework to create a worksheet before class. Alternatively, you could improvise by asking students to suggest ideas for the game; for example, *Find someone who has a big family / a computer in his or her room*.

WORK WITH WORDS Parts of the body

1

- Read the instructions aloud and refer students to the pictures.
- Have students look at the PHRASE BYTES box and explain that these are useful phrases for giving opinions.
- Divide the class into pairs and have students discuss the question. Then invite them to share their opinions with the class.

2a ▶31

- Ask a student to read the instructions aloud and check that students understand the task.
- Play the track for students to listen and point to the parts of the body in the pictures.
- If students need to listen again, play the track again, pausing after each word to check that students can find it.
- Ask students to do the Words & Beyond exercise on page 57.

AUDIO SCRIPT ▶31

Mandy: These are my new pictures.
Sam: Wow! They're really original. Arm … hand … leg … foot … back … head … . Great idea.
Mandy: Thanks. The face picture is a little hard to read.
Sam: Let me look … face … ear … mouth … teeth … eye … nose …. It's fine. Really cool.

2b ▶32

- Play the track for students to listen and repeat the words.

AUDIO SCRIPT ▶32

See Student's Book, page 22, for audio script.

Extra activity

For extra practice with parts of the body, play a game of *Simon Says* … (See Teaching Tips, *Total Physical Response*, page 24.) Before starting the game, preteach any instructions that students might not know; for example, *shake* (*your head*), *touch* (*your feet*), *put up* (*your arm*), *wave* (*your hands*). Remind students to do the action only if you start the sentence with *Simon says …*

3a

- For this activity, students will need colored pencils, crayons, or markers. They will need the colors red, blue, pink, green, and yellow.
- Divide the class into A/B pairs and read the instructions aloud.
- Have Student As read the description on page 61 and dictate it for Student Bs to draw the picture.
- Set a time limit of three minutes for the task.
- Stop the activity and ask students to hold up their pictures to compare them as a class.

3b

- Ask students to read the instructions. Have Student Bs read the description on page 62 and dictate it for Student As to draw the picture. Repeat the procedure for Exercise 3a.

Extra activity

For extra practice, have students play another variation on *Picture Dictation* (see Games, page 29). Rather than using a written description as in Exercise 3, ask students to draw their own monsters, and encourage them to make their monsters very strange. Set a time limit of three minutes for students to draw their pictures. When they've finished, have them take turns describing their pictures for their partners to draw.

SPEAK AND LISTEN

4

- Ask students to look at the title of the quiz and the photos. Explain that this is a quiz – a game where you have to answer questions. Elicit some examples of TV or radio quiz shows that students watch or listen to.
- Ask a student to read the instructions aloud, and then divide the class into pairs.
- Set a time limit of three minutes for students to do the quiz.
- Stop the quiz, but don't check answers at this point, as students are going to listen and check their answers in Exercise 5.

ANSWERS

1 B   2 B   3 A   4 B   5 C

5 ▶33

- Ask a student to read the instructions aloud.
- Play the track for students to listen and check their answers from Exercise 4.
- Invite students to share their answers with the class. The winners are the pairs with the most correct answers.

ANSWER / AUDIO SCRIPT 33

The winner is Kim.

Host: Welcome to *Whose is it?* Today we have a quiz on famous parts of the body. And to play we have Kim ...
Kim: Hello.
Host: ... and Alan.
Alan: Hi.
Host: Welcome to *Whose is it?* Let's start. Picture 1 ... a mouth. Whose is it?
Kim: Um, I think it's Shakira's mouth.
Host: No, I'm afraid that's wrong. It isn't hers. It's not really the mouth, it's the smile ... it's the Mona Lisa's mouth. ... Next picture. Ah, yes ... two white hands.
Alan: Are they Mickey Mouse's hands?
Host: Good try ... Mickey has white hands, but they aren't his. They're Mario's hands – from the Super Mario games ... . Picture 3. A soccer player's legs. Do you have any ideas?
Alan: That's easy. They're Balotelli's legs. They're fantastic with a soccer ball!
Host: Correct! Yes, Mario Balotelli's legs. ... Picture 4. Ah ... a funny ear.
Kim: It's Mr. Spock's ear. He has funny ears like that.
Host: Correct! It's Mr. Spock's ear from *Star Trek*. ... OK, Picture 5. A brown eye with a lot of makeup?
Kim: Lady Gaga ... she has brown eyes, and she always wears a lot of makeup.
Host: Correct! Yes, it's Lady Gaga's eye. And the winner is ... Kim! Congratulations.

6 33

- Read the instructions aloud and refer students to the examples.
- Play the track for students to listen and answer the questions.
- Let students compare their answers in pairs before you check them as a class.

ANSWERS / AUDIO SCRIPT 33

2 *His hands are* white.
3 His legs are fantastic with a soccer ball.
4 His ears are funny.
5 Her eyes are brown with a lot of makeup.

See Exercise 5 for audio script.

Alternative procedure: less confident classes

The recording of the quiz show might be more challenging than some students are used to, so for less confident classes, hand out copies of the audio script the second time students listen. Explain that they can read along if they want to.

REACT

7

- Read the instructions aloud and refer students to the PHRASE BYTES box. Point out that we use *have* to talk about parts of the body. Elicit some other possible sentences; for example, *I have green eyes. My mom has green eyes too.* Model the phrases and have students repeat them.
- Divide the class into pairs and ask students to discuss the questions. Set a time limit of two minutes.
- Monitor and note errors and good use of language to go over in a feedback session at the end of the activity.
- Stop the activity and invite several students to tell the class what they found out about their partners.
- Give feedback on good language and errors.

MOVE BEYOND

Ask students to do the Words & Beyond exercise on page 57.

MOVE BEYOND FOR TEACHERS

Teaching parts of the body

In some younger classes, students may get embarrassed or overexcited by discussion of bodies and parts of the body. Think about the maturity and sensitivity of your group, and try to anticipate their reaction and how you'll deal with it. Ignoring their response is always a possibility, although it can be argued that where there's an emotional response, there's greater student engagement. In this case, you might want to laugh along with the jokes or teach some more personal parts of the body. However, if you choose to do this, make sure it's done in a sensitive manner that doesn't offend anyone (students, parents, other teachers, etc.).

Homework

Ask students to create their own quiz like the one in Exercise 4. Suggest that they find the parts of the body from five pictures of famous people on the internet or in magazines, and that they write a multiple-choice question with three options for each one. In the next class, divide the class into small groups and have students ask and answer the questions in each other's quizzes.

GRAMMAR *Whose?*; possessive *'s/s'* and possessive pronouns

Talk about your things, family, and friends *Page 23*

STAGE	TIME	FOCUS
GET STARTED		Play a guessing game to review possessive adjectives and test knowledge of possessive *'s/s'* and possessive pronouns.
READ AND LISTEN		Read and listen to a conversation about a vacation photograph.
STUDY		Use the conversation to help you complete examples with possessive forms.
PRACTICE		Practice using *whose*?, possessive *'s/s'*, and possessive pronouns in controlled exercises.
SPEAK		Play a game to practice using possessive *'s/s'* and possessive pronouns.

Get started

In order to review possessive adjectives and test what students know about the target structures in the lesson, play a game where students have to guess whose things are whose. You will need to bring two large bags to class. Divide the class into two groups and give a bag to each group. Ask everyone to put something of theirs in the bag (e.g., a watch, a scarf, etc.) and to switch bags with the other group. Then explain that students should take turns taking something from the bag, and their group should try to guess whose it is. Model an example, and then play the game as a class. As they play, draw students' attention to any good use of possessive *'s/s'* and possessive pronouns.

READ AND LISTEN Grammar in context

1 ▶34

- Have students look at the photo and ask *What can you see? Where are the people?*
- Read the instructions aloud and check that students understand the question.
- Play the track for students to listen, read, and think about the answer to the question.
- Call on several students to give their answers. Ask them to give reasons for their answers.

ANSWER / AUDIO SCRIPT ▶34

The (nice) legs on the left.

See Student's Book, page 25, for audio script.

STUDY

2

- Read the instructions aloud and have students complete the table with words from Exercise 1. Circulate and give help as necessary.
- Let students compare their answers in pairs before you check them as a class.
- At this point, you might want to highlight the difference between possessive *'s* and the short form of *is* – *'s*. Borrow something from a student (e.g., a pen), and write two sentences with blanks on the board; for example, *Carla ______ pen is on the desk. It ______ blue.* Elicit from students that *'s* goes in both blanks. Then elicit that in the first sentence *'s* is the possessive *'s*, and in the second, it is the verb *be*.
- Refer students to the **Grammar Database** on page 53 and see Teaching Tips, *Possessive adjectives and possessive pronouns,* page 25.

ANSWERS

brothers' Whose

3

- Read the instructions aloud and ask the class to identify the possessive adjectives in column 1. Check that students remember all of the possessive adjectives by eliciting a sentence for each; for example, *Whose pen is this? It's her pen.*
- Have students complete the table with words from Exercise 1.
- Let students compare their answers in pairs before you check them as a class.
- Refer students to the **Grammar Database** on page 53.

ANSWERS

yours his Theirs

Extra activity

If you allow students to use cell phones in class, divide the class into two groups and have students take a photo of all the feet in their group. The photo could be similar to the one in Exercise 1, although they don't need to take their shoes off! Then ask the groups to trade phones and say whose feet they can see. Encourage them to use the language from Exercises 2 and 3.

PRACTICE

4

- Ask students to look at the pictures and say what parts of the body they can see.
- Read the instructions aloud and refer students to the example.
- Ask students to complete the sentences with *'s* or *s'* and a part of the body.
- Let students compare their answers in pairs before you check them as a class.

ANSWERS

2 my brothers' arms
3 my grandparents' feet/legs
4 my grandpa's teeth
5 my friends' hands
6 my mom's foot

5

- Ask students to skim the conversation to find out what things are mentioned. Tell them not to worry about the blanks.
- Check ideas as a class. Then read the instructions aloud and have students complete the conversation. Remind them to refer to the grammar explanation in Exercise 3.
- Let students compare their answers in pairs before you check them as a class.

ANSWERS

2 mine 3 theirs 4 his 5 ours 6 yours

Fast finishers

Ask fast finishers to look at the quiz on page 22 and to write two sentences for each of the pictures, one with possessive *'s* and one with a possessive pronoun; for example, *That's the Mona Lisa's mouth. That mouth is hers.* Note that in this case, where the sense of distance is subjective, students can use *this/that* and *these/those* interchangeably. To avoid confusion, accept either possibility in students' sentences.

SPEAK

6

- Have a student read the instructions aloud, and check that students understand the game. Remind them to use possessive *'s* and possessive pronouns.
- Have students stand up and play the game. To liven up the game, you could play music when students are moving around (as in the game *Musical Chairs*) and stop it when they sit down in a chair. Make sure students have enough space to move around the classroom without bumping into each other.

Homework

Ask students to draw or take photos of things that belong to their family and friends (e.g., their dad's chair, their sister's bike, etc.). Ask them to choose six things, and on the back of the paper or photo, to write a couple of sentences to say whose it is and something about it. Encourage them to use possessive *'s/s'* and possessive pronouns where possible. In the next class, divide the class into pairs and have students ask each other questions to find out who the things belong to.

Be friendly to other students

Page 24

STAGE	TIME	FOCUS
GET STARTED		Talk about what a friend is.
READ		Read and listen to a conversation between two girls. Say what they have in common.
DO		Read tips about making friends. Put them in order and match them to examples.
REFLECT		Talk about your friends and making friends.
EXTEND		Make new friends in class. Find out about their families and their interests.

SCHOOL SKILLS

BE FRIENDLY TO OTHER STUDENTS

The value of friendship in teenagers is generally taken for granted. Research suggests that it can, among other things, help them:

- develop social skills.
- learn to control emotions.
- feel more positive about school.
- build self-esteem.
- learn about relationships.
- develop new interests.

All of these benefits are felt not only in childhood but also in adult life, helping to define us emotionally, socially, and morally. It is therefore important for a class to have a friendly atmosphere and for students to be encouraged to make friends.

Get started

In order to set up the topic for the lesson, write the question *What's a friend*? on the board. Brainstorm a couple of ideas; for example, *They help you with your homework, They share things with you,* and start a list on the board. Then ask students to think of more ideas and give them a minute or two to think about it. Divide the class into pairs and ask students to make a list of their ideas. Circulate and give help as necessary, and when each pair has two or three ideas, invite students to come to the board and add their ideas to the list. To conclude, ask students to decide as a class which ideas are the most important.

READ

1 35

- Ask students to look at the picture and describe what they can see (e.g., *two girls talking, a school bag*, etc.). Teach any words students are unsure about (e.g., *lockers*).
- Ask a student to read the instructions aloud. Then play the track for students to read and listen to the conversation.
- Invite students to share their answers with the class.

ANSWER / AUDIO SCRIPT 35

High School Story is their favorite movie.

See Student's Book, page 24, for audio script.

Extra activity

Ask students to close their books and make two columns in their notebook with the headings "Tina" and "Helen." Divide the class into pairs and ask them to write down everything they can remember about the two girls. Elicit a couple of examples; for example, *Tina has one sister* and *Helen's in the movie club*. Set a time limit of two minutes for this. Then stop the activity and ask students to open their books and compare their ideas. Invite students to say how many things they remembered correctly.

DO

2

- Read the instructions aloud and call on a student to read the tips in the "Make Friends" box aloud.
- Divide the class into pairs and ask them to order the tips. Remind them to use the conversation in Exercise 1 to help them.
- Call on students to share their answers with the class, and ask them to match the tips to a part of the conversation in Exercise 1; for example, d – *Hello. I'm Tina.*

ANSWERS

1 d 2 c 3 e 4 b 5 a

3

- Read the instructions aloud and elicit the answer to number 1. Point out that some tips may be used more than once.
- Ask students to match the sentences to the tips in Exercise 2.
- Let students compare their answers in pairs before you check them as a class.

ANSWERS

1 c 2 e 3 a 4 d 5 b 6 b

REFLECT

4

- Read the instructions and the questions aloud.
- Call on students to read the expressions in the PHRASE BYTES box aloud.
- Divide the class into small groups for students to discuss the questions using the expressions in the PHRASE BYTES box.
- Set a time limit of two minutes for the task. Then stop the activity and invite students to share their answers with the class. As this may be a sensitive issue for some students, have students speak only if they want to.
- Ask a student to read the REFLECTION POINT aloud, and ask the class whether they agree or disagree, encouraging them to give reasons.

EXTEND

5a

- Tell students that they're going to try to make new friends in the class and that they're going to think about things to talk about.
- Read the instructions aloud and give some examples of questions they could ask; for example, *Do you have any brothers or sisters? What's your favorite TV show?*
- Set a time limit of two minutes for students to write their questions. Circulate and give help as necessary.

5b

- Have a student read the instructions aloud and check that students understand the task.
- Set a time limit of five minutes for students to walk around and ask each other their questions. Encourage them to talk to classmates they do not know well.
- Monitor and note errors and good use of language to go over in a feedback session at the end of the activity.
- Stop the activity and invite students to share what they learned about their classmates before giving feedback yourself on good language and errors.

Alternative procedure: less confident classes

Before starting the activity in Exercise 5a, ask less confident classes to look at the conversation in Exercise 1 and to underline the questions. Invite students to come up to the board and write the questions. Brainstorm variations on the questions; for example, *What's your favorite soccer team? What's your email address?* etc. Encourage students to refer to the board to help them with ideas for their questions.

Homework

Ask students to write an article for a website about how to make friends. Ask them to write about 50 words and to include ideas of their own. In the next class, ask students to exchange their articles and compare their ideas.

SPEAKING On the phone

Talk on the phone *Page 25*

STAGE	TIME	FOCUS
GET STARTED		Review and practice saying phone numbers.
SPEAK		Talk about the telephones your family has.
LISTEN		Listen to three phone conversations and complete them with phrases for talking on the phone (speaking subskill). Practice the conversations.
ACT		Act out different phone conversations.

Get started

The lesson focuses on phone conversations, so this lead-in reviews how to say phone numbers. Prepare five phone numbers and explain that you're going to say some phone numbers for students to write down. Make sure that some of the numbers include 0. When you've dictated the numbers, let students compare their answers in pairs before calling on students to come to the board and write the phone numbers. Ask students how we say *0* (*oh*) and elicit that we say each number individually (e.g., *4-1-2-5-3-2-0*). Ask students to practice reading the numbers on the board. If you feel that it's appropriate, you could then have students exchange their own phone numbers in pairs to add to their contact lists. If not, they could invent phone numbers to practice asking and answering about phone numbers in small groups.

SPEAK

1

- Read the questions aloud. Then divide the class into pairs and have students answer the questions.
- Invite students to share their answers with the class. You could do a survey to find out how many students have cell phones and which families have the most phones.

LISTEN

2 36

- Call on a student to read the instructions and the situations aloud. Then ask students to cover the texts.
- Play the track for students to listen and match the situations to the conversations.
- Ask students to read the conversations to check their answers, and then let them compare their answers in pairs.
- Call on students to share their answers with the class.

ANSWERS / AUDIO SCRIPT 36

1 C 2 A 3 B

1

Felix: Hello?
Mrs. Zemontas: Hi, Felix. This is Mrs. Zemontas. Can I speak to your mother?
Felix: She isn't here right now.
Mrs. Zemontas: OK, can she call me, please? It's Emily Zemontas.
Felix: Um ... Can you spell that, please?
Mrs. Zemontas: Z-E-M-O-N-T-A-S.
Felix: OK, Mrs. Zemontas.
Mrs. Zemontas: Thanks, Felix. Bye.

2

Felix: Hel–
Kelly: Hi, are you at the movies?
Felix: Sorry, I don't understand. What movie?
Kelly: Is this Josh?
Felix: No, it isn't. You have the wrong number.
Kelly: Oh, I'm sorry. Bye.

3

Felix: Hello?
Mark: Hi, Felix, this is Mark. Is Kyle there?
Felix: No, he isn't.
Mark: Can you give him my new cell phone number?
Felix: Sure.
Mark: It's 830-0315.
Felix: 830 ... Sorry, can you repeat that?
Mark: 830-0315.
Felix: 830-0315. OK.
Mark: Thanks. Bye.

3a 36

- Call on a student to read the instructions aloud. Then play the track again for students to listen and complete the conversations.
- Let students compare their answers in pairs, but don't check answers at this point.

ANSWERS / AUDIO SCRIPT 36

See underlining in audio script in Exercise 2.

3b 37

- Play the track for students to listen and check their answers to Exercise 3a.
- Call on students to share their answers with the class. Then play the track again for students to listen and repeat the sentences.
- As students are doing this, draw attention to the rising intonation in the requests.

AUDIO SCRIPT 37

1 Can I speak to your mother?
2 Can she call me, please?
3 Can you spell that. please?
4 Sorry, I don't understand.
5 You have the wrong number.
6 Sorry, can you repeat that?

4

- Read the instructions aloud, and then divide the class into pairs for students to practice the conversations.
- Allow two or three minutes for them to practice. Then invite pairs to act out the conversations for the class.

ACT

5 38

- Read the instructions aloud and give students a minute or two to read through the situations. Check that they understand all of the situations.
- Refer the class to the PHRASEBOOK and call on students to read the useful phrases aloud. Then play the track for students to listen and repeat.
- Divide the class into A/B pairs and have students sit back-to-back in order to simulate the conditions of a phone call.
- Set a time limit of five minutes for students to act out the conversations and remind them to use the phrases from the PHRASEBOOK in their conversations.
- Monitor and note good use of language and errors for feedback at the end of the task.
- Stop the activity and focus on the good language and errors that you noted. Then invite pairs to act out the conversations for the class.

Extra activity

So that students have the chance to practice the conversations with different classmates, have them sit in two concentric circles with half the class in the inside circle facing in and the other half in the outside circle with their backs to them. Explain that the students in the inside circle are Student A and those on the outside are Student B, and that they have only one minute to act out each conversation. Read aloud the notes for conversation 1 and have students act out the phone call with the person behind them. After one minute, have the students on the outside move one place to the left and then repeat the activity for the remaining conversations.

Homework

Ask students to think of famous people and to write two phone conversations similar to the ones in Exercise 2. Elicit some ideas for celebrities, what they might say, and their situations. For example, it could be Justin Bieber calling to speak to Miley Cyrus, but her mom answers the phone. Refer students to the expressions from the PHRASEBOOK and ask them to write four to six lines for each conversation. In the next class, have students practice and act out the conversations with a partner.

WRITING My favorite person

Write a description of a person Page 26

STAGE	TIME	FOCUS
GET STARTED		Talk about important people in your life.
READ		Describe people in pictures. Read a description of a person and learn how to use apostrophes (writing subskill).
PRACTICE		Complete a text with apostrophes.
DISCUSS		Describe an important person in your life.
WRITE		Write a description of an important person in your life.
SHARE		Listen to your classmates' descriptions. Name an interesting thing about each person and say which person you want to meet.

Get started

In order to prepare students for the topic of the lesson and to provide an opportunity for reviewing family words, write the names of six people who are important to you on the board, (e.g., mother, best friend, neighbor, etc.). Then explain that students have to find out who the people are by asking Yes/No questions; for example, *Is Paul your brother?* When students have found out who the people on your list are, have them make their own lists. Divide the class into groups of three or four and have them find out who the people on the lists are.

READ

1

- Ask a student to read the instructions and the words in the box aloud. Check pronunciation of the words and drill as necessary.
- Divide the class into pairs and ask them to describe the people. Remind them to use the words in the box and *have* (e.g., *She has gray hair*), and set a time limit of two minutes.
- Monitor and note good use of language and errors for a feedback session at the end of the task.
- Stop the activity and invite students to share their ideas with the class. Then give feedback on good language and errors.

2

- Read the instructions aloud and point out that students should underline the important words that help them match the description to a picture.
- Set a time limit of two minutes for students to match the description to one of the pictures.
- Let students compare their answer in pairs before you check it as a class. Ask them to give reasons for their choice by referring to the words they underlined.

ANSWERS
Picture 2
Important words: friendly, black and gray hair, small nose

3

- Call on a student to read the tips in the HOW TO box aloud. Point out that a word with a missing letter replaced by an apostrophe is called a contraction and that possessive *'s/s'* goes with a noun.
- Ask students to look back at the description in Exercise 2 and to circle all the words with apostrophes. Then have them work with a partner to decide which are for missing letters (contractions) and which are possessive *'s/s'*.
- Check answers as a class.

Extra activity

To clarify the difference between *it's* and *its*, tell students that you're going to describe a city and they have to guess which one. Read the following description of New York aloud: *It's very big and its inhabitants are from all over the world. Its restaurants are very expensive and its nickname is "the Big Apple." It's a popular tourist destination.* Alternatively, use any big city that you think students will recognize from its description. Let students discuss their ideas in pairs before you check the answer as a class. Ask students which were the important words (e.g., *big, "Big Apple"*). Then ask them to reconstruct the description using *it's* and *its*. Circulate and give help as necessary before inviting students to reconstruct the text on the board. Time permitting, you could ask students to write their own descriptions of another city.

ANSWERS
dad's = possessive She's = She is She's = She is
I'm = I am It's = It is

PRACTICE

4

- Read the instructions aloud and have students read through the text quickly. Ask them what they can remember about the writer; for example, *She has a brother and two sisters.*
- Read the first sentence aloud and, as an example, ask students where to put an apostrophe (*brother's*).
- Have students put the apostrophes in the rest of the description. Remind them to refer to the HOW TO box.
- Let them compare their answers in pairs before you check them as a class.

ANSWERS
brother's brother's sisters' aren't

DISCUSS

5

- Explain that students are going to describe an important person in their lives. Go over the instructions and give them a few minutes to think of a person and to make some notes if they want to.
- Divide the class into pairs and set a time limit of three minutes for them to describe their important people to each other. Circulate and give help with vocabulary as necessary.

WRITE

6

- Tell students that they are going to write a description of the person they described in Exercise 5. Go over the instructions in Exercise 6 and check that students understand the three points. Remind them to refer back to the paragraph in Exercise 2 and to the HOW TO box.
- Set a time limit of 10 minutes for writing. Circulate, giving help as necessary.
- When students have finished writing, ask them to check their descriptions to make sure they have followed all the instructions correctly.

SHARE

7

- Divide the class into small groups. Ask students to read their descriptions aloud to their groups. Tell them to make a note of one interesting thing about each person described and to decide which person they want to meet.
- Call on several students to say which person they want to meet and to share one interesting thing about that person.

Homework

Invite students to think of a famous person they like, such as a pop star, sports star, scientist, etc. Ask them to write a description (about 60 words) of that person, but tell them not to include the person's name. Remind them to use descriptive adjectives and to refer to the Words & Beyond section on page 57. In the next class, have students display their descriptions around the classroom for other students to guess who the people are.

VOCABULARY Family

1

- Ask students to look at the photo and elicit ideas about Hakan and who he is (*a young Turkish-American pop star*). Encourage students to discuss what family members they can see.
- Ask students to complete the description of the photo. Point out that some of the letters of each word are given and that there's one blank for each letter.
- Let students compare their answers in pairs before you check them as a class.

ANSWERS
1 mother 2 father 3 mom 4 dad 5 grandmother
6 grandfather 7 Grandma 8 Grandpa 9 grandchild
10 only child 11 brothers 12 sisters

Parts of the body

2

- Refer students to the words in the box and the picture.
- Ask students to write the parts of the body.
- Let students compare their answers in pairs before you check them as a class.

ANSWERS
1 head 2 face 3 eye 4 nose 5 mouth 6 teeth
7 ear 8 back 9 arm 10 hand 11 leg 12 foot

GRAMMAR *Have*

3

- Explain that students are going to read an interview with Hakan talking about his house.
- Ask students to read the text through quickly without worrying about the blanks.
- Ask students to complete the interview with *have* and *do, does,* or *don't*.
- Let students compare their answers in pairs before you check them as a class.

ANSWERS
1 have 2 Does (it) have 3 does 4 has 5 have
6 Do (you) have 7 don't

Whose?; possessive *'s/s'* and possessive pronouns

4

- Ask students to look at the conversation and choose the correct options to complete it. Suggest that they read through the text first to help them understand.
- Let students compare their answers in pairs before you check them as a class.

ANSWERS
1 Whose 2 mom's 3 hers 4 mine 5 friends'
6 theirs

SKILLS CHECK

- Ask students to think about what they've learned in this unit and to check the sentences.
- Divide the class into pairs to discuss what they've learned, and use this as an opportunity to review anything students still have difficulties with.

Extra Resources

Go to the Teacher's Resource Center at mee2.macmillaneducation.com for:

- downloadable audio and audio scripts for the Student's Book and Workbook
- videos, video worksheets, and video scripts
- extra vocabulary at two levels of difficulty
- extra grammar at two levels of difficulty
- CLIL lessons, with full teacher's notes
- school skills lessons, with full teacher's notes
- Speaking Database materials
- the *Move Beyond Intro A Level* wordlist
- downloadable PDF and Word tests for Unit 2 (all skills)
- tips for using the Grammar Database
- extra reading materials
- and more!

Go to the Workbook pages 82–93 for further practice material.

PROGRESS CHECK UNITS 1&2

Preparing for the Progress Check

The Progress Check can be done either as a review of the two preceding units or as a formal test. For the first one, it's a good idea to encourage students to prepare as thoroughly as they can so that they get into the habit of regularly reviewing what they have learned. Reassure the class that the Progress Check contains only material that they have covered in the previous two units.

Ask students what advice they would give to a friend who was about to take a test. Students should be able to come up with tips such as *Read the instructions carefully*; *Don't worry about words you don't know.* Write these on the board before asking the class to vote on the most important tip.

Vocabulary review

- Draw a table on the board with the following headings: *Things, Countries and nationalities, Family, Parts of the body.*
- Invite students to come to the board and write vocabulary items under each heading; as they do this, check that everyone remembers the items. The list does not need to be complete.
- With several items in each column, refer students to the Unit Reviews on pages 17 and 27. Encourage them to call out any items they missed. Students can then go through the Progress Check and see how many of the items they can find.

Grammar review

- Remind students that they studied a number of grammar points on pages 11, 13, 21, and 23. Start a "race," where students tell you the main grammar points from each unit (Unit 1: Plural nouns; *a/an, the*; *This/that, these/those*; Unit 2: *Have*; *Whose?*; possessive *'s/s'* and possessive pronouns). Write these on the board, asking for examples as students call them out.

Optional warm-up activities

These activities are suitable when you are not using the Progress Check as part of a formal test. They are low-risk activities to encourage full group participation, and they are designed to help students focus on the tasks and to guide them toward performing better in the Progress Check. This is particularly important in a less confident class where students need extra help with techniques and how to approach exam tasks.

READ Exercise 1

- Have students look at Exercise 1 in the Progress Check and ask the following questions: *How many conversations can you see?* (*six, including the example conversation*); *What kind of questions are they?* (*multiple-choice questions*); *How many answer choices are there?* (*three*).
- Refer students to the first part of the conversations and ask them to say which one:
  says something nice (3)
  asks a question about your family (1)
  asks for information about you (4)
  is the answer to a phone call (5)
  asks about things around you (2)
- Point out the importance of looking carefully at the verb in each question before making your answer choice. Remind students that adjectives help us understand whether it's a positive or negative situation. For example, in question 3, the speaker says *nice*, which helps us understand that he or she likes the bag.
- Going through the example together should help students gain confidence to attempt the rest on their own. If they find it difficult, encourage students to look at the first question with a partner.

LISTEN Exercise 2

- Refer students to Ivy's notes. Inform them that they can find a lot of useful information before they start listening. Illustrate this by asking the following questions:
  What is the phone call about? (*a drama group*)
  What do we know? (*It's on Saturday morning, the place starts with the word* Victoria, *the teacher is female* – Ms.)
  How many things does Ivy have on her list? (*six*)
- Divide the class into pairs or small groups and ask them to predict what question words they think they will hear for each of the things on the list. After two or three minutes, call on students around the class to say the question words they expect to hear (e.g., *How many, How old, Where, What, What*).

WRITE Exercise 3

- Write the following on the board: *m* _ _ _ _
  Ask students how many letters are missing (*four*); they don't need to guess the word yet. Remind students that one line is one letter.
- Write on the board: *You speak with this.* Ask students to complete the word for the part of the body (*mouth*).
- Ask students to think of descriptions for *nose* and *leg*; for example, *You smell with this*; *You walk with these.* Point out to students that this activity will help them answer the questions in Exercise 3.

WRITE Exercise 4

- Refer students to the HOW TO boxes on pages 16 and 26. Make sure they understand the importance of including these grammar points in their writing.
- Ask students to write their names and three questions about family and friends with the structures *Do you have … ?*; *How old … ?*; *Can you tell me about … ?* on a piece of paper. Collect the pieces of paper and ask different students some of the questions.

Doing the Progress Check

READ Exercise 1

- If you have decided not to do the full warm-up, focus students' attention on the example and ask them to say why the answer is C (*The question starts with* Whose … ? *and so the answer contains a possessive pronoun)* and can't be the other two options (*Option A is incorrect because* her *is a possessive adjective, not a possessive pronoun, and Option B is incorrect because* book *is singular, not plural).*
- Go through the **Test-Taking Tips** with the class and make sure they understand how to answer multiple-choice questions.
- Allow 10 minutes for this section.

ANSWERS
1 A 2 B 3 C 4 B 5 B

LISTEN Exercise 2

39

- If you have decided not to do the full warm-up, divide the class into pairs and ask students to spend a minute or two predicting the questions Ivy might ask for each item on the list and the possible answers.
- Make sure they understand that they have to listen for specific information and write the answers next to each number.
- Go through the **Test-Taking Tips** for the listening task, briefly referring students back to the work they did on page 25.
- Point out that they will hear everything twice.
- Allow 10 minutes for this section.

ANSWERS / AUDIO SCRIPT 39

1 14 2 13 3 School 4 Campbell 5 820-4577

Ivy: Hi, Alec.
Alec: Oh hi, Ivy.
Ivy: I need more information about the drama group so I can talk to my mom about it.
Alec: Sure. Well, we meet every Saturday.
Ivy: In the morning or in the afternoon?
Alec: In the morning. For two hours.
Ivy: OK. How many people are in the group?
Alec: Mmm ... 15, I think. No, 14. There are 14.
Ivy: How old are the other people?
Alec: They're all 13. Like us.
Ivy: And where is it?
Alec: It's at Victoria School. The drama teacher is really good.
Ivy: What's her name?
Alec: Ms. Campbell.
Ivy: Campbell? Can you spell that, please?
Alec: C-A-M-P-B-E-L-L.
Ivy: Um, OK. Do you have her phone number? Then my mom can call her.
Alec: Just a minute ... yes, here it is. It's 820-4577. Do you have that?
Ivy: 828 ... 4577.
Alec: No, eight two *zero* ... four five seven seven.
Ivy: OK, I have it. Thanks a lot, Alec. See you at school.
Alec: See you, Ivy. Bye.

WRITE Exercise 3

- Go through the **Test-Taking Tips** for this task. Make sure students understand that they have to write one letter on each line.
- Focus students' attention on the example and ask them what vocabulary is being tested here (*Parts of the body*). Briefly refer students back to the work they did on page 22.
- Explain that spelling is important for this task and that on a test they would lose credit for spelling mistakes. Remind students to pay careful attention to whether the word is singular or plural.
- Allow five minutes for this section.

ANSWERS

1 eyes 2 hands 3 teeth 4 feet 5 face

WRITE Exercise 4

- Since this is the first test of students' writing, spend a few minutes going through the task with them, eliciting who they're writing to (*Jason*) and what their message should include (*information about members of their family: how many people, brothers and sisters, ages, and descriptions*).
- Remind students that even if their writing is excellent, they won't get full credit if they don't include all the points.
- Refer students back to the writing activities and the HOW TO boxes on page 16 and page 26. Stress the importance of correct word order in a sentence or phrase with adjectives.
- Go through the **Test-Taking Tips** for this task. Elicit from students what the word limit is (*25–35 words*) and remind them to check their spelling and grammar when they've written their texts.

MODEL ANSWER

I have a small family. I have a mom and dad, two grandmas, and a sister. Grandma Schumacher is German. My sister's 14. She's quiet and very smart. She has brown eyes.

After the Progress Check

Optional game

This game will help lighten the atmosphere after the Progress Check, and it follows up on the vocabulary and grammar covered in it.

- Write 10 things about yourself in clouds on the board; for example:

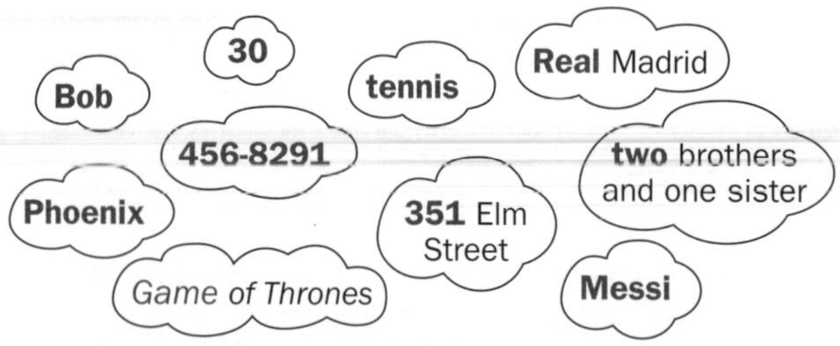

- Put students in pairs and ask them to guess the questions to the answers on the board; for example, *What's your name? How old are you? What's your hobby? What's your favorite soccer team? Where are you from? What's your telephone number? Do you have any brothers or sisters? What's your favorite TV show? What's your address? Who's your favorite soccer player?*
- Now ask students to write five surprising things about themselves that their classmates might not know in five clouds. Put them back in their pairs and tell them to ask each other a question for each piece of information. Invite students to say what they learned about their partners.

Feedback and extension

After the Progress Check has been graded, provide feedback to the class as a whole and individually as far as possible. Ask students which parts they found the most difficult and how they think they could improve their grades next time.

READ Exercise 1

- Review the conversations one at a time and encourage students to say why the other options are wrong. Where there were mistakes, find out whether the problems were in understanding the questions or the answers.
- Encourage students to read in English as much as they can. Graded Readers are an excellent tool to improve vocabulary, sentence structure, and all reading skills. Students can read them in the classroom or at home. Visit www.macmillanreaders.com for information about available titles and support material to help you use graded readers in class.

LISTEN Exercise 2

- Handing out photocopies of the audio script is a good way to provide feedback. Deal with any mistakes in this way. Seeing the conversation written down helps students recognize when they've misheard something. It will also help them become aware of distractors.

WRITE Exercise 3

- Students who struggled in Exercise 3 need to review the vocabulary for *Parts of the body*. Write *feet* and *teeth* on the board and elicit the singular nouns for these words. If necessary, ask students to review this vocabulary and test it again at the beginning of the next class.

WRITE Exercise 4

- For students who had difficulty with Exercise 4, change the message to a similar task; for example, *Tell me about your class. Do you have a big or a small class? Do you have any good friends in your class? Tell me about them.*
- Build up a written text together on the board. You could write this yourself, based on suggestions, or invite individual students to come to the board and write a sentence each.

3 UNIT ANIMAL MAGIC

IN THE PICTURE Adopt a pet

Talk about pets

Pages 30–31

STAGE	TIME	FOCUS
GET STARTED		Play a game to practice saying letters of the alphabet and lead in to the topic of the unit.
WORK WITH WORDS		Review parts of the body. Learn and practice using vocabulary for pets. Practice pronunciation of the short /ɪ/ sound. Watch a video of animals, write the names of the animals, and count them.
WRITE AND SPEAK		Talk about pets.

Get started

In order to lead in to the topic of the unit – animals – in a fun way, play a game of *Snowman* (see Games, page 29) with famous cartoon and movie animals. First, ask students to think of a famous animal (e.g., Mickey Mouse, Pingu, etc.), and then play once as a class to make sure students understand the game. Divide the class into groups of four to play the game, circulating and helping students with pronouncing the letters as necessary. Stop the activity after five minutes and ask students what famous animals they thought of. Elicit the types of animals they are (or tell them) and write them on the board (e.g., *mouse, penguin*, etc.).

WORK WITH WORDS Pet animals

1 RECALL

- Ask a student to read the instructions aloud. Refer students to the example and elicit another example.
- Divide the class into pairs and set a time limit of one minute for them to write the parts of the body.
- Call on students to share their answers with the class.
- Ask students to do the Work with Words task on page 58.

SUGGESTED ANSWERS

back eye face foot head leg mouth nose

2a

- Point out that the animals in the pictures are pets and elicit the meaning of *pet*.
- Read the instructions aloud and set a time limit of two minutes for the task.
- After two minutes, let students compare their answers in pairs, but don't check them at this stage.

2b ▶40

- Play the track for students to listen and check their answers to Exercise 2a. Then call on students to share their answers with the class.
- Play the rest of the track for students to listen and repeat the words.

ANSWERS / AUDIO SCRIPT ▶40

bird a cat j chicken e dog h fish b hamster c horse d mouse f rabbit g turtle i

bird cat chicken dog fish hamster horse mouse rabbit turtle

Extra activity

To give students extra practice in saying the words, divide the class into A/B pairs. Tell Student As to close their books and try to recall all the animals in the same order as they are in the book. Tell Student Bs to listen and if Student A makes a mistake, to switch roles.

MOVE BEYOND FOR TEACHERS

Adopt a pet

In many countries, it's now very popular to adopt a pet rather than buying one. Organizations and charities often have websites where you can find the right pet for you. This means that animals that might otherwise be homeless can be matched with a new owner. In this lesson, the text and pictures show a similar website. If you have access to the internet in your classroom, you might want to show your students an authentic website and have students search for animals they'd like to adopt.

3a

- Point out that the pictures are from a website about pets and refer students to the tablet with the *Adopt a Pet* website.
- Read the instructions aloud and have students read the first description and match it to an animal.
- Check ideas as a class. Then have students match the rest of the descriptions to animals.
- Let students compare their answers in pairs, but don't check them at this point.

3b ▶41

- Play the track for students to listen and check their answers to Exercise 3a.

ANSWERS / AUDIO SCRIPT ▶41

1 horse
2 dog
3 chicken
4 cat
5 bird

4a ▶42

- Ask a student to read the instructions aloud. Refer students to the example and remind them to use the animals from Exercise 2a.
- Play the track for students to listen and write the animals.
- Let students compare their answers in pairs before you check them as a class.

ANSWERS / AUDIO SCRIPT ▶42

2 fish 3 turtle 4 mouse 5 hamster

1
Julia: This is my pet rabbit, Harvey. He has very, very big ears. He's three years old, and he's a very happy rabbit.

2
Brian: Um ... this one's name is Happy, and that one's Grumpy. Where's Smiley? Ah! There he is! I have a lot of fish. It's hard to remember their names.

3
Karen: This is Terry. My pet turtle's eight years old. Look! He has small eyes and a big mouth. He loves the water!

4
Leo: So her name is Minnie ... you know, Minnie's the name of Mickey Mouse's girlfriend? She's very small. She likes to sit on my hand. She's a good mouse.

5
Nicky: I think it's a Russian hamster. It doesn't have a name. It's brown, and it has a black line down its back.

4b ▶42

- Read the instructions aloud and give students a minute to read the questions.
- Play the track for students to listen and answer the questions.
- Let students compare their answers in pairs before you check them as a class.

ANSWERS / AUDIO SCRIPT ▶42

2 Julia's pet has big ears
3 Karen's pet has small eyes.
4 Nicky's pet doesn't have a name.

See Exercise 4a for audio script.

Alternative procedure

Before playing the track, you could ask students if they remember the answers and ask them to discuss them in pairs. Invite students to share their ideas with the class. Then play the track to check their answers.

5a ▶43 PRONOUNCE

- Read the instructions aloud and model the /ɪ/ sound. Point out that it's a short sound. (See Teaching Tips, *Long and short vowel sounds*, page 28.)
- Play the track for students to listen and repeat the words.

AUDIO SCRIPT ▶43

See Student's Book, page 30, for audio script.

b ▶44

- Play the track for students to listen and repeat the words.

AUDIO SCRIPT ▶44

See Student's Book, page 30, for audio script.

Extra activity

For further practice of the /ɪ/ sound, write the following short conversations that recycle vocabulary from Unit 1 on the board:

- *Who visits Pittsburgh?*
- *Tourists visit Pittsburgh.*

- *Where's the little dog?*
- *In the living room.*
- *It isn't in the living room.*
- *Oh! It's in the kitchen.*

Invite students to come to the board and underline the /ɪ/ sounds. Give students a couple of minutes to practice the conversations in pairs, and then invite several pairs to present them for the class.

6 THE MOVING PICTURE ▶

- Ask a student to read the instructions aloud.
- Play the video for students to watch and write the animals they see.
- Play the video again for students to watch and count how many animals there are.
- Let students compare their answers in pairs before you check them as a class.

ANSWERS / VIDEO SCRIPT

There are 10.

1 fish (two) 2 cat (one) 3 dogs (five) 4 hamster (one)
5 horses (four) 6 mice (two) 7 birds (three)
8 turtle (one) 9 rabbit (one) 10 chickens (12)

There is no dialog in this video.

WRITE AND SPEAK

7a

- Read the instructions aloud and model the task by choosing an animal and writing some notes on the board.
- Give students two minutes to complete the form.

7b

- Read the instructions aloud and refer students to the useful phrases. Model this stage of the task by referring to your notes on the board and telling students about your pet.
- Divide the class into pairs and have students tell each other about their pets. Ask them to take notes about their partners' pets so they can tell the class at the end. Set a time limit of three minutes.
- Monitor and note good use of language and errors for feedback at the end of the task.
- Invite students to tell the class about their partners' pets. Then give feedback and correct errors.

MOVE BEYOND

Ask students to do the Words & Beyond exercise on page 58.

Homework

Ask students to write an email (about 60 words) to a friend telling him or her about their new pet. Ask them to use their notes and the useful phrases from Exercise 7 and to refer to the adjectives in the Words & Beyond section on page 58.

At the beginning of the next class, have students compare their emails in small groups and decide whose pet they like the most.

READING Teach your pet English

Read instructions *Page 32*

STAGE	TIME	FOCUS
GET STARTED		Review and practice classroom instructions.
SPEAK AND READ		Talk about your pets. Learn how to use pictures to help you understand new words in a text (reading subskill). Read a web page and act out the instructions in the article.
REACT		Talk about pets in your country and how you communicate with them. Write the orders and instructions from the web article in your own language.

Get started

As the text focuses on instructions, take the opportunity to review classroom instructions. Write some examples of classroom instructions on the board; for example, *Open/Close your books; Stand up*. Divide the class into small groups and ask students to brainstorm more classroom instructions. Set a time limit of two minutes. Then stop the activity and invite students to come to the board and write their ideas. Model and drill the expressions, and then have students take turns giving each other instructions; for example, one student says *Stand up*, and the others in the group stand up. Model a couple of examples with the class, and then give students two minutes to practice.

SPEAK AND READ

1

- Read the instructions and questions aloud and refer students to the useful phrases in the PHRASE BYTES box.
- Give students a minute to think about the questions and to take notes.
- Divide the class into pairs and set a time limit of three minutes for the task. Remind students to use the useful phrases.
- Monitor and note good use of language and errors for feedback at the end of the task.
- Invite students to tell the class about each other's pets. Then give feedback on good language and errors.

2 45

- Refer students to the **Reading Tip** and then ask them to look at the web page and say what it is for (*teaching your pet English*). Ask students how the pictures helped them; for example, *There are pictures of a person telling a dog to do different things in English.*
- Ask a student to read the instructions aloud and set a time limit of two minutes for students to answer the question. Don't play the audio at this point. It is an extra feature, and a suggestion for using it in class is included at the end of the lesson.
- Let students compare their answers in pairs before you check them as a class.

ANSWERS

The orders and instructions aren't for all kinds of pets.
Always be nice to your pet.
It's important to say the orders in the right way.

Extra activity

Write the following words from the picture captions on the board: *Here, Sit, Stay, Down, Up, Quiet, No, Shake, Fetch*. Divide the class into pairs and give them a minute to look at the pictures and captions. Then tell them to close their books and try to write the full instruction for each word; for example, *Here* = *Come here*. Then have them check their work with the captions.

3

- Explain the miming activity and mime one of the orders on the web page as an example. Ask students to say the order you are miming without looking at their books.
- Divide the class into pairs. Tell Student As to choose any three of the instructions in any order and mime them for Student Bs to guess the instructions with their books closed. Then have them switch roles for the other three orders.
- At the end of the activity, ask students which orders are difficult to remember. You could take the opportunity to suggest some ways to remember new words. (See Teaching Tips, *Remembering new words*, page 25.)

REACT

4

- Read the instructions and the questions aloud. Then refer students to the useful phrases in the PHRASE BYTES box. Elicit some possible endings for the phrases.
- Give students a minute to think about their answers, and then divide the class into pairs to ask and answer the questions.
- Discuss the questions as a class. Ask students if they would like to use the instructions from the web page with their pets. If they say yes, challenge them to try it!

MOVE BEYOND

Ask students to write the orders and instructions from the article in their own language.

Recorded reading text 45

Tell students that they are going to listen to a recording of the web page and practice saying the orders. Ask students to listen and read. Then play the track again, pausing after each of the orders for students to repeat them. Remind students that the web page says it's important to say the instructions in the right way, so they should copy the intonation as closely as possible. Congratulate students who say the orders well and invite them to repeat the orders for other students to copy them.

Homework

Ask students to create a similar web page for classroom instructions. Ask them to include at least six classroom instructions and pictures to illustrate them. At the beginning of the next class, have students display their web pages around the classroom and let them move around and say which web pages they like the best.

GRAMMAR Imperatives and object pronouns

Give orders and instructions

Page 33

STAGE	TIME	FOCUS
GET STARTED		Unscramble words to review pet vocabulary.
READ AND LISTEN		Read and listen to a conversation about a new pet.
STUDY		Complete examples with imperatives and object pronouns.
PRACTICE		Practice using imperatives and object pronouns in controlled exercises.
SPEAK		Play a game to practice giving and following instructions.

Get started

Review the pet words from pages 30–31 by writing the following scrambled words on the board (answers in parentheses):

shore (horse) *hifs (fish)* *drib (bird)* *thrames (hamster)* *ogd (dog)* *tac (cat)* *rtutel (turtle)* *ousem (mouse)* *kencich (chicken)* *birbat (rabbit)*

Explain that the scrambled letters are all words for pet animals and that students have to write the correct words. Elicit the first word from the class. Divide the class into small teams and set a time limit of three minutes for them to write all the words. Stop the activity and check answers as a class, awarding one point for each correct word. The team with the most words is the winner.

READ AND LISTEN Grammar in context

1a

- Ask students to look at the picture and describe what they can see (*a young girl looking excited about something*).
- Call on a student to read the instructions aloud. Then have students read the text and answer the question.
- Let students compare their ideas in pairs. Remind them to give reasons for their answers. Don't check the answer at this stage.

1b 46

- Play the track for students to listen and check their answer. Then check the answer as a class.

ANSWER / AUDIO SCRIPT 46

a hamster

See Student's Book, page 33, for audio script.

Extra activity

Have students practice and act out the conversation. Divide the class into groups of three and choose students in each group to play Mom, Dad, and Laura. Give students a couple of minutes to practice their parts and then have them act out the conversation in their groups before inviting some groups to act it out for the class.

STUDY

2

- Read the instructions aloud and explain that imperatives are used for orders and instructions.
- Refer students to the examples in the table and focus on form by asking *What verb form is it?* (*base form*); *What word do we use when it's negative?* (*don't*).
- Ask students to find more imperatives in the conversation to complete the table.
- Let students compare their answers in pairs before you check them as a class.
- Refer students to the **Grammar Database** on page 54.

ANSWERS

Find Don't put

3

- Refer students to the table and point out the example. Explain that we use an object pronoun in place of a noun and that it goes after a verb or a preposition. If necessary, give more personalized examples; for example, say to a student *Give me your pen*; *Speak to her*; etc. Write some sentences with noun objects on the board and ask students to rephrase the sentences with object pronouns.

- Ask students to find more object pronouns in the conversation to complete the table.
- Check answers as a class, and then refer students to the **Grammar Database** on page 54.

ANSWERS
me you him her it us them

PRACTICE

4

- Refer students to the tips and point out that *tips* are suggestions for how to do something.
- Set a time limit of three minutes for students to choose the correct options to complete the sentences.
- Let students compare their answers in pairs before you check them as a class.

ANSWERS
2 Be 3 Give 4 Don't say 5 Play
6 Don't take

5

- Read the instructions aloud and ask students to look at the signs. Ask them to cover the sentences and encourage them to say what the signs mean.
- Ask students to uncover the sentences and set a time limit of two minutes to match the sentences to the signs.
- Let students compare their answers in pairs before you check them as a class.

ANSWERS
2 e 3 d 4 a 5 b

Fast finishers
Ask fast finishers to guess where you can see the signs (e.g., in the street, in a park, etc.). Ask them to write down their ideas. Elicit their ideas as you check the answers to Exercise 5.

6

- Read the instructions aloud and go over the example. Encourage students to read the sentences before writing the pronouns and to refer to the table in Exercise 3.
- Set a time limit of three minutes for the exercise and circulate and give help as necessary.
- Let students compare their answers in pairs, and then call on students to share their answers with the class.

ANSWERS
2 it 3 them 4 him 5 her 6 us

SPEAK

7

- Read the instructions aloud and go over the examples. Choose a student to model the activity with.
- Divide the class into pairs and set a time limit of three minutes for the activity. Make sure there's space in the classroom for students to move around. Circulate and help students with ideas.
- You might want to finish up the activity with a class game of *Simon Says …* .

Homework

Ask students to look back at the conversation in Exercise 1 and elicit the ideas that Mom and Dad give Laura for taking care of her pet; for example, *Don't put him in your room*; *Give him food and water every day*; etc. Ask students to think of another pet and to rewrite the conversation with different advice. Ask them not to write the name of the animal but to leave a blank. At the beginning of the next class, have students read each other's conversations and guess what animal it is.

LISTENING AND VOCABULARY A new neighbor

Listen to a description of a room Page 36

STAGE	TIME	FOCUS
GET STARTED		Play a game to find out how confident students are with prepositions of place and to review imperatives.
WORK WITH WORDS		Learn and categorize vocabulary for things in a room.
SPEAK AND LISTEN		Listen to a description of a room and identify the room (listening subskill).
REACT		Talk about your favorite room.

Get started

In this lesson, students listen to a conversation about things in a room. Prepositions of place, *in*, *on*, and *next to* appear in the recording, so to prepare students and find out what they know, give them instructions using prepositions; for example, *Put your pen on your desk*; *Sit next to a different student*; etc. When students seem confident carrying out the instructions, call on different students to give instructions. This activity also provides a useful review of imperatives.

WORK WITH WORDS Things in your room

1

- Read the instructions aloud. Then refer students to the PHRASE BYTES box and explain that they are useful phrases for answering the questions.
- Divide the class into pairs and give students a couple of minutes to ask and answer the questions. Then invite them to share their answers with the class.

ANSWERS
cat, dog, birds, dinosaur

2a

- Call on two students to read the instructions and the words in the box aloud.
- Set a time limit of two minutes for students to match the things in the pictures to the words in the box.
- Let students compare their answers in pairs, but don't check them at this stage.

2b 47

- Play the track for students to listen and check their answers.
- Then play the second part of the track for students to listen and repeat the words. Highlight the stress on the longer words (e.g., *computer*, *picture*, *window*).

ANSWERS / AUDIO SCRIPT 47

bed e chair f clock d computer i desk h door a
floor c light b picture k table l wall g window j

bed chair clock computer desk door floor light
picture table wall window

3

- Read the instructions aloud. Then refer students to the examples and elicit another example for each category.
- Set a time limit of two minutes for students to categorize the words.
- Let students compare their answers in pairs before you check them as a class.
- Ask students to do the Words & Beyond exercise on page 58.

ANSWERS

Parts of a room: *door*, floor, wall, window
Furniture: *bed*, chair, desk, table,
Other things: *clock*, computer, light, picture

Extra activity

For extra practice, have students take turns covering the words in the box, pointing to an object in the rooms, and asking *What's that?* for a partner to say the correct word.

SPEAK AND LISTEN

4 48

- Read the instructions aloud and point out that students have to identify one of the two rooms in Exercise 1.
- Explain that they will hear an animal talking because the track is a cartoon, which is a film of animated drawings. Play the track for students to listen and decide which room is being described.
- Call on a student to share the answer with the class.

ANSWER / AUDIO SCRIPT 48

Room 2

Dog: A little more ... OK! Stop!
Cat: So? What can you see?
Dog: It's a room.
Rabbit: Excuse me.
Cat: Yes ... And?
Dog: There's a window.
Cat: Of course there's a window. You're looking in it!
Dog: And there's a bed. There's a small table next to the bed with a light on it.
Rabbit: Um... Excuse me!
Horse: Are there any pictures?
Dog: Yes, Horse. There are some pictures on the walls.
Rabbit: Excuse me, but I can't....
Dog: There's a door. No, wait... There are two doors. And there's a desk with a computer.
Cat: Is he there?
Dog: Who?
Cat: The new neighbor!
Dog: Yes! He's on the floor.
Rabbit: Hello-o?
Cat: What is it, Rabbit?
Rabbit: I ... I ... I'm sorry!

5a 48

- Call on students to read the instructions and questions aloud.
- Play the track for students to listen and answer the questions.
- Let them compare their answers in pairs, but don't check them at this point.

AUDIO SCRIPT 48

See Exercise 4 for audio script.

5b

- Ask students to look at the picture on page 61 and check the answers as a class. Ask students what animals they can see and if they are surprised.

ANSWERS

1 pet animals 2 a dog 3 the animals fall

Extra activity

Hand out copies of the audio script and divide the class into groups of four. Assign a role (cat, dog, horse, and rabbit) to each student and have them practice and act out the conversation. Encourage them to act like those animals by making animal noises, etc.

6a

- Read the instructions aloud and point out that the sentences are excerpts from the conversation in Exercise 4.
- Set a time limit of two minutes for students to complete the sentences with words from the box in Exercise 2.

6b 49

- Let students compare their answers in pairs before you play the track for them to listen and check their answers.
- Call on students to share their answers with the class.

ANSWERS / AUDIO SCRIPT 49

2 table 3 light 4 pictures 5 doors
6 desk 7 floor

See Student's Book, page 36, for audio script.

REACT

7

- Have a student read the instructions and the questions aloud and refer students to the PHRASE BYTES box. Model some possible answers using the phrases; for example, *My favorite room is my bedroom. There's a big table with a computer on it, and there's a nice bed. My cat is on the bed.*
- Divide the class into pairs and have students ask and answer the questions. Set a time limit of two minutes.
- Monitor and note errors and good use of language to go over in a feedback session at the end of the activity.
- Invite students to tell the class about their partner's favorite room.

MOVE BEYOND

Ask students to do the Words & Beyond exercise on page 58.

Alternative procedure: more confident classes
Have students circulate and ask different students the questions. Set a time limit of five minutes for students to talk to as many classmates as possible and to take notes on their answers. Then divide the class into small groups to talk about the favorite rooms of the people they talked to. At the end of the activity, take a class survey to find out what the most popular rooms are.

Homework

Ask students to start a new vocabulary section in their notebooks about things in a room. Ask them to think of another room in their house and to draw a plan of that room. Then ask them to label the things in that room. Encourage them to use dictionaries and the internet to find out new words. At the beginning of the next class, have students show each other their rooms and ask questions about the things in them; for example, *What's that? What are those?*

GRAMMAR *There is / there are*

Describe a room

Page 35

STAGE	TIME	FOCUS
GET STARTED		Play *Kim's Game* to review *there's a/an* and vocabulary from previous lessons.
READ AND LISTEN		Read and listen to a conversation about classrooms.
STUDY		Complete grammar explanations with examples of *there is / there are*.
PRACTICE		Practice using *there is / there are* in controlled exercises.
SPEAK		Draw a plan of your room and ask questions about your partner's room to make a list of what's in it.

Get started

In order to review *there's a/an*, which appeared in the PHRASE BYTES box in the previous lesson and which will be developed in this lesson, play *Kim's Game*. As students have seen only the singular form (*There's*), objects should be singular. Prepare around 10 small items (e.g., *a card*, *a glass*, *a label*, etc.). Cover the items and tell students they will have one minute to look at them and memorize what they see without writing anything down. Reveal the items for one minute. So that students have to use the target language, divide the class into pairs to discuss the objects they saw and remind them to use *There's a* … .

READ AND LISTEN Grammar in context

1 50

- Have students look at the picture and ask what they can see. Elicit that the girl has a clipboard for a survey and that the survey is about classrooms.
- Read the instructions aloud and check that students understand the question.
- Play the track for students to read and listen to the conversation to find out what's wrong with the computer room.
- Let students compare their answer in pairs before you check it as a class.

ANSWER / AUDIO SCRIPT 50
There aren't any windows.
See Student's Book, page 35, for audio script.

Extra activity 50
Have students cover the conversation and ask them to remember what's in Mario's classroom. Set a time limit of two minutes for this. Then ask students to uncover the conversation. Play the track for them to listen, read, and check their answers before you check answers as a class.

ANSWERS
a table a chair desks for the students windows
pictures on the wall a clock a door

STUDY

2a

- Refer students to the table and point out that when we describe things in a place (e.g., a room, school, house, etc.), we use *there is* for singular things and *there are* for plural things.
- Read the instructions aloud and ask students to refer to the conversation to help them complete the examples in the table.
- Call on students to share their answers with the class and point out the use of contractions and of *some/any* for plural nouns.
- Refer students to the **Grammar Database** on page 54.

ANSWERS
aren't is aren't

2b

- Read the instructions aloud and elicit some examples. Point out that students have to underline more examples in the conversation.
- Set a time limit of two minutes. Then let students compare their examples in pairs before you check them as a class.

ANSWERS
Natalie: What's your English classroom like?
Mario: It's OK. There's a table and a chair for the teacher. There are desks for the students. There are some windows. Oh, and there are some pictures of the USA and the UK on the wall, but there isn't a picture of Australia.
Natalie: Is there a clock?
Mario: Yes, there is. It's next to the door. Why?

Natalie:	The questions are for a school survey. Are there any computers?
Mario:	No, there aren't. There are computers in the computer room. I don't like the computer room. There aren't any windows.

Extra activity
Have students circle the questions in the conversation and then ask each other the questions about their own classroom. Remind students to use *there is/are* and to refer to the table in Exercise 2a. Monitor and note good language and errors for feedback at the end of the task.

PRACTICE

3

- Ask students to look at the picture and say what they can see in the classroom.
- Read the instructions aloud and refer students to the example.
- Ask students to decide if the sentences are correct or not and to rewrite the incorrect sentences.
- Let students compare their answers in pairs before you check them as a class.

ANSWERS
2 C
3 I – There isn't a clock on the wall.
4 I – There are two doors.
5 C
6 I – There are seven computers.

4

- Read the instructions aloud and refer students to the example. Elicit the second question.
- Ask students to write the remaining questions and then to ask and answer the questions in pairs.
- Check the questions and answers as a class.

ANSWERS
2 Are there any windows?
3 Is there a table for your teacher?
4 Are there any pictures on the wall?
5 Is there a bed?
6 Are there any computers?

5

- Ask students to look at the conversation and read it quickly without worrying about the blanks. Then ask them who's talking (*Natalie and Mario*) and what about (*his room*).
- Ask a student to read the instructions aloud and refer students to the example.
- Set a time limit of three minutes for the task and ask students to complete the conversation with the correct forms of *there is / there are*.
- Let students compare their answers in pairs before you check them as a class.

ANSWERS
2 Is there 3 there isn't 4 Are there
5 There are 6 there is

SPEAK

6

- Have a student read the instructions aloud and check that students understand the tasks.
- Set a time limit of three minutes for students to draw the plan of their room. Then divide the class into pairs. Remind students not to show their plans to their partners.
- Read the instructions for the second task aloud again and refer students to the useful phrases. Model an example by choosing a student and asking some questions about his or her room. Write some of the things on the board.
- Set a time limit of three minutes for students to ask questions and make a list of the things in their partners' rooms.
- Monitor and note good use of language and errors for feedback at the end.
- Stop the activity and ask students to compare their lists with their partners' plans. Then invite students to tell the class about their partners' rooms.
- Give feedback on good language and errors.

Homework

Explain that students are going to write a description of their room for a website. Ask students to write a description (about 60 words) using their room plan from Exercise 6. Remind students to use *there is/are* and *some/any*. At the beginning of the next class, divide the class into small groups to read each other's descriptions and find things in common.

LANGUAGE & BEYOND *SCHOOL SKILLS*

Prepare your things for school

Page 36

STAGE	TIME	FOCUS
GET STARTED		Play a game of *What's in the bag?* to find out what people have in their backpacks.
SPEAK AND READ		Talk about pictures. Read statements and match them to the pictures.
DO		Say how you prepare for school and where you keep things. Decide whether you do things at the best time and keep things in good places.
REFLECT		Talk about how to prepare for school.
EXTEND		Think of tips to help students organize their things and be ready for each class.

SCHOOL SKILLS

PREPARE YOUR THINGS FOR SCHOOL

In this lesson, students think and talk about how they prepare for school and how to organize their time. Teenagers are not known for their organizational skills, and this is particularly true of younger students who have just started in secondary school. Therefore, it's helpful to show students the value of organization, especially when it comes to preparing for school. We can point out that being organized helps reduce stress and allows students to use their time more efficiently. We can also remind them that time saved in preparing for school and tests means more free time!

Get started

Play a game of *What's in the Bag?* First, make sure that you have a range of different objects in your bag and remove anything you don't want students to see. Then invite them to come up and put their hands in the bag, pick an object, and try to guess what it is without looking at it. Put some phrases for speculating on the board to help them; for example, *I think it's a ... ; I'm not sure*. After you've modeled the activity with a few students, divide the class into two groups and have students play the game with their own backpacks. Set a time limit of two minutes, and then ask students to say what things they have in their backpacks.

SPEAK AND READ

1a

- Read the instructions aloud. Refer students to the PHRASE BYTES box and point out that they saw these structures in the last lesson.
- Divide the class into pairs. Tell them to look at the pictures for one minute.
- Have students close their books and make lists of all the things they can remember.

1b

- Have students open their books and compare their lists with the pictures.
- Ask students which things are difficult to remember and suggest ways to remember them. (See Teaching Tips, *Remembering new words*, page 25.)

Extra activity

Ask students to think of other things they might find on a desk (e.g., *laptop*, *calculator*, *ruler*, etc.). Divide the class into pairs and challenge students to think of as many things as they can in one minute. Then have pairs work in groups of four to compare their lists.

2

- Read the instructions aloud and refer students to the example. Elicit reasons for the example; for example, *A and B are before school because both clocks say 6:30*.
- Divide the class into pairs and give students a couple of minutes to discuss the statements. Encourage them to give reasons for their answers.
- Check answers as a class and ask students which desk they prefer.

ANSWERS

2 B 3 A 4 B

DO

3a

- Read the instructions aloud and elicit answers from several students.
- Give students a minute to choose their answers, and then have them discuss their answers in pairs. Encourage them to give their reasons; for example, *I prepare lunch before bed because I don't have time in the morning.*

Extra activity

To extend and personalize the task, refer students to the list of things students do to prepare for school. Then brainstorm more ideas as a class (e.g., *take a shower*, *charge my phone*). Encourage students to say when they do each thing.

3b

- Read the instructions aloud and give students a minute to think about their answers. Then have them discuss their answers in pairs. Encourage them to give their reasons; for example, *I keep my keys in my backpack because I don't need them at school.*

4

- Call on a student to read the instructions aloud. Divide the class into pairs and have students discuss their answers to Exercises 3a and 3b and then discuss the questions.
- Invite the class to discuss the best time to do the activities in Exercise 3a, where they keep the things in Exercise 3b, and whether they are good places. Encourage students to give reasons for their opinions.

REFLECT

5

- Call on students to read the instructions and questions aloud. Then refer the class to the useful phrases in the PHRASE BYTES box. Elicit that *ready* means *prepared*.
- Divide the class into small groups and set a time limit of three minutes for students to discuss the questions. Circulate and give help as necessary.
- Stop the activity and invite students to share their answers with the class.
- Ask a student to read the REFLECTION POINT aloud and then ask students if they agree with the advice and to give their reasons.

EXTEND

6

- Read the instructions aloud and elicit what *tips* means (*good suggestions*).
- Divide the class into pairs and give students a couple of minutes to think of their tips.
- Invite students to share their tips with the class and to decide which tips are the best.

Homework

Ask students to make a poster with tips on how to prepare things for school. Encourage them to include the things from Exercise 3 and their tips from Exercise 6 and to illustrate the poster. At the beginning of the next class, you could display the posters around the classroom and ask students to choose the best ones.

SPEAKING You're welcome

Ask for and give things

Page 37

STAGE	TIME	FOCUS
GET STARTED		Write a description of a room and match descriptions to pictures to review vocabulary for things in a room and *there is / there are*.
SPEAK		Look at pictures and say what you can see.
LISTEN		Listen to three conversations and complete them. Study uses of *have* and *borrow* and learn polite phrases (speaking subskill).
ACT		Act out different conversations where you ask for things politely.

MOVE BEYOND FOR TEACHERS

Politeness

This lesson presents situations where people are requesting things and where politeness is important. Although some people say English is a "polite language," politeness is a feature of all languages; however, ways of being polite differ and are often complex areas for learners. It's therefore a good idea to introduce students to key concepts from the beginning (e.g., the use of modals like *can* and *could*, words like *please* and *thank you*, and rising intonation). Encourage students to use new expressions and strategies at every opportunity and provide help for less confident students by having a section on the board with useful phrases; for example, *Can I go to the restroom, please?* (See Teaching Tips, *Being polite*, page 26.)

Get started

In order to review vocabulary for things in a room and *there is / there are*, first prepare various pictures of rooms, either from magazines and catalogs or from the internet. Divide the class into pairs and give one picture to each pair. Ask them to write a short description of the room and remind them to use *there is / there are* and to refer to the vocabulary from page 34. Then display the pictures around the classroom and give the descriptions to different pairs of students. Explain to students that they have three minutes to walk around the classroom and find the picture that matches the description they have.

SPEAK

1

- Read the instructions aloud and refer students to the PHRASE BYTES box.
- Divide the class into pairs and have students describe what they can see in the pictures.
- Call on students to share their answers with the class.

LISTEN

2a

- Call on a student to read the instructions aloud. Then ask students to use the pictures to help them complete the conversations.
- Don't check answers at this point, as students will listen and check their answers in Exercise 2b.

2b 51

- Play the conversations for students to listen and check their answers to Exercise 2a.
- Call on students to share their answers with the class.

ANSWERS / AUDIO SCRIPT 51

See underlining in audio script below.

1
Jeff: Can I have some water, please?
Lisa: Yes, of course. Here you are.
Jeff: Thanks.
Lisa: You're welcome.

2
Mia: Excuse me. Can I borrow your pen?
Brett: Sure. Here you are.
Mia: Thanks.
Brett: You're welcome.

3
Amy: Hi, Kevin. Can I borrow your phone?
Kevin: No, sorry.
Amy: Oh. OK.
Donna: You can borrow mine.
Amy: Thanks, Donna.
Donna: You're welcome.

3

- Read the instructions aloud and have students complete the sentences.
- Let students compare their answers in pairs before you check them as a class. Make sure they understand the meaning of *borrow*.

ANSWERS

1 borrow 2 have

4 52

- Explain that students are going to listen to some phrases from the conversation for asking for things and responding.
- Play the track for students to listen and repeat the phrases.
- While students are doing this, draw attention to the rising intonation in the requests and ask them which words are stressed.

AUDIO SCRIPT 52

1 Can I have some water, please?
2 Excuse me. Can I borrow your pen?
3 Yes, of course.
4 No, sorry.
5 Here you are.
6 Thanks.
7 You're welcome.

5 (▶53)

- Call on a student to read the instructions aloud. Then set a time limit of two minutes for students to put the sentences in the right order.
- Let students compare their answers in pairs. Then play the track for them to listen and check.
- Check answers as a class.

ANSWERS / AUDIO SCRIPT (▶53)

Kevin: Dad? Can I have some money?
Dad: No, sorry.
Kevin: Please, Dad!
Dad: OK. Here you are.
Kevin: Thank you.
Dad: You're welcome.

Alternative procedure: less confident classes
Less confident groups might find the jumbled conversation a little difficult, so to get them started and limit the options, elicit the first two lines of the conversation. Then circulate and help students as they reorder the rest of the conversation.

Extra activity
Divide the class into pairs and ask students to practice the conversations in Exercises 2a and 5. Give students three minutes to practice, and then invite some pairs to act out the conversations for the class.

ACT

6 (▶54)

- Explain that students are going to prepare two conversations and give them a moment to read through the instructions. Refer students to the PHRASEBOOK and play the track for them to listen and repeat the phrases.
- Divide the class into pairs and set a time limit of five minutes for students to write and practice the conversations. Remind them to use *have* and *borrow* and the phrases from the PHRASEBOOK.
- Circulate and help with ideas and language.
- Have the pairs work with another pair. Ask them to act out their conversations for the other pair.
- At the end of the activity, ask several pairs how their conversations were different from those of the other pair.

Homework

Ask students to write a jumbled conversation like the one in Exercise 5. Explain that the conversation should have six lines and should use new language from the lesson. At the beginning of the next class, have students work in pairs and reorder each other's conversations.

WRITING Don't forget

Write a note *Page 40*

STAGE	TIME	FOCUS
GET STARTED		Play a game to review imperatives.
READ		Read different notes. Match them to pictures and answer questions. Learn tips for how to write a note (writing subskill).
PRACTICE		Identify the important words in notes.
DISCUSS		Talk about work you do at home and instructions your parents give you.
WRITE		Write a note giving instructions.
SHARE		Read your note to other students. Decide who has the clearest instructions.

Get started

In this lesson, students are asked to write notes and use imperatives. To review imperatives and giving instructions, write the following sentences on the board:

a Wait for a few minutes.
b Eat it alone or share it with friends!
c Put it in the oven.
d Turn off the oven.
e Put it on a plate.
f Turn on the oven.
g Take it out of the box.
h Take it out of the oven.

Explain that they are the instructions for cooking food and ask students to guess the food (*pizza*). Elicit the meaning of *oven*, *plate*, and *box*. Then ask students to work in pairs and put the instructions in the correct order. Check the answer as a class.

ANSWER
The correct order is f, g, c, a, h, d, e, b.

READ

1

- Ask students to look at the pictures and talk about what they can see.
- Have students read the notes and match them to the pictures.
- Call on students to share their answers with the class.

ANSWERS
1 b 2 c 3 a

2

- Read the instructions aloud and ask students to answer the questions.
- Let students compare their answers in pairs before you check them as a class. When checking answers, ask students to give their reasons and ask extra questions to check comprehension; for example, *Where's the pizza? What time does William call Barbara?*

ANSWERS

1 She's at Grandma's house.
2 pizza
3 Harry's a cat.
4 on the table
5 It's for his son, William.
6 6 p.m.

3

- Ask a student to read the tips in the HOW TO box aloud and refer students to the **Grammar Database** on page 54 for more information about imperatives.
- Ask students to look at the notes again and circle the imperatives.
- Let students compare their answers in pairs before you check them as a class.

ANSWERS

(Be) good.
(Don't forget!)
(Give) Harry ....
(Call) Barbara ... .

PRACTICE

4

- Read the instructions aloud and do the first sentence as an example.
- Ask students to underline the important words in the other two notes.
- Let them compare their answers in pairs before you check them as a class.

ANSWERS

1 Class C: German class is in Room 17 today.
2 Dear Hilary, Enjoy your vacation. Please write and send me a postcard.
3 Don't forget to put the keys on the table for your aunt and uncle.

Extra activity

To help consolidate the structures seen in the lesson, have students reconstruct the notes from Exercise 4. When checking answers, invite students to write the important words on the board, and then ask students to help you reconstruct the notes. Do the first one as an example. Then divide the class into pairs, if possible pairing more confident with less confident students, and set a time limit of five minutes for the task. Circulate and help students as necessary. To check their notes, have the class help you reconstruct the notes on the board.

DISCUSS

5

- Give students a couple of minutes to think about what work they do at home and to think of answers to the questions. Tell them to also think about what instructions their parents give them for doing these things.
- Divide the class into pairs and ask them to talk about the work they do at home and the instructions their parents give them.

WRITE

6

- Explain to students that they are going to write a note giving someone instructions. Go over the three steps with them and then give them a couple of minutes to think about what they want to write.
- Set a time limit of five minutes for writing, and remind students to follow the three steps and to refer to the tips in the HOW TO box. Circulate and help as necessary.
- When students have finished writing, ask them to check their notes to make sure they've followed the steps and answered all the questions.

SHARE

7

- Divide the class into groups and ask students to read their notes aloud. Tell them to decide who has the clearest instructions. At the end of the activity, you may want to have the students who wrote the clearest instructions read their notes to the class.

Homework

Tell students that an American friend is staying with them. They're at school, so they're going to leave a note for their friend to suggest things to do. Ask students to think of three things to do and two things not to do. Brainstorm some ideas as a class; for example, *go to the movies – there's a good movie, eat lunch – there's spaghetti in the refrigerator, don't eat the chocolate – it's my mom's!* Ask students to write 30–40 words and to refer to the tips in the HOW TO box. Point out that they can use *Dear* ... to start the note and to write their name at the end. At the beginning of the next class, have students share their notes with other students to compare their ideas.

VOCABULARY Pet animals

1

- Ask students to look at the web pages on the page and point out that they are all from a website for a pet hotel.
- Ask students to look at the pictures in Exercise 1 and write the words. Tell them that the first letter of each word is given and that there is one blank for each letter.
- Let students compare their answers in pairs before you check them as a class.

ANSWERS
1 dog 2 rabbit 3 cat 4 mouse 5 bird
6 turtle 7 hamster 8 chicken 9 fish 10 horse

Things in your room

2

- Refer students to the text and elicit that it is the information page of the pet hotel's website.
- Ask students to choose the correct options to complete the text. Encourage them to read through the text first.
- Let students compare their answers in pairs before you check them as a class.

ANSWERS
1 walls 2 door 3 window 4 floor 5 bed
6 table 7 light 8 chair 9 desk 10 computer
11 clock 12 picture

GRAMMAR Imperatives and object pronouns

3

- Refer students to the text and elicit that it is the home page of the pet hotel's website.
- Ask students to complete the text with the words and phrases in the box.
- Encourage them to read through the text first.
- Let students compare their answers in pairs before you check them as a class.

ANSWERS
1 Don't stay 2 Come 3 you 4 Eat 5 him
6 them 7 Don't forget 8 us

There is / there are

4

- Point out that this is the questions page of the website.
- Ask students to match the sentence halves.
- Let students compare their answers in pairs before you check them as a class.

ANSWERS
1 d 2 c 3 a 4 f 5 b 6 e

SKILLS CHECK

- Ask students to think about what they've learned in this unit and to check the sentences.
- Divide the class into pairs to discuss what they've learned, and use this as an opportunity to review anything students still have difficulties with.

Extra Resources

Go to the Teacher's Resource Center at mee2.macmillaneducation.com for:

- downloadable audio and audio scripts for the Student's Book and Workbook
- videos, video worksheets, and video scripts
- extra vocabulary at two levels of difficulty
- extra grammar at two levels of difficulty
- culture lessons, with full teacher's notes
- school skills lessons, with full teacher's notes
- Speaking Database materials
- the *Move Beyond Intro A Level* wordlist
- downloadable PDF and Word tests for Unit 3 (all skills)
- tips for using the Grammar Database
- extra reading materials
- and more!

Go to the Workbook pages 94–105 for further practice material.

UNIT 4 PLAY

IN THE PICTURE Free time

Talk about your free-time activities

Pages 40–41

STAGE	TIME	FOCUS
GET STARTED		Play a game to review free-time words.
WORK WITH WORDS		Review and learn new words and phrases for free-time activities. Match them to photos and practice saying them. Watch a video and write the free-time activities.
WRITE AND SPEAK		Talk about your favorite free-time activities.

Get started

Play a game of *Picture Dictation* (see Games, page 29) with free-time words. At this point, use words like *soccer, movies, book,* etc., rather than verb phrases, as these are studied in the lesson.

WORK WITH WORDS Free-time activities

1 RECALL

- Read the instructions aloud and explain that students have to find free-time words in the grid. Point out the clue and encourage students to use the pictures to help them find the words.
- Divide the class into pairs and set a time limit of three minutes.
- Stop the activity and check answers as a whole class.
- Ask students to do the Work with Words task on page 59.

ANSWERS

B	H	X	M	O	V	I	E	S	B	T	B
I	S	H	O	P	P	I	N	G	O	E	M
K	E	D	A	V	V	N	P	P	O	L	U
E	T	B	D	B	U	R	B	R	K	E	S
X	S	O	C	C	E	R	L	L	C	V	I
V	I	D	E	O	G	A	M	E	S	I	C
G	C	Y	C	O	I	B	I	N	X	S	K
F	R	I	E	N	D	S	B	B	L	I	W
X	V	V	A	N	P	X	Z	Y	M	O	K
A	R	I	N	T	E	R	N	E	T	N	X

2 55

- Go over the instructions and divide the class into pairs. Set a time limit of three minutes for students to match the free-time activities to the verbs. Remind students to use the words from Exercise 1.
- Play the track for students to listen and check their answers. Then call on students to give the answers.
- Continue the track for students to listen and repeat the activities.

ANSWERS / AUDIO SCRIPT 55

1 *go shopping* 2 go to the movies 3 go on the internet
4 listen to music 5 meet friends 6 play soccer
7 play video games 8 read a book 9 ride my bike
10 watch television

go shopping go to the movies go on the internet
listen to music meet friends play soccer play video games
read a book ride my bike watch television

3 56

- Read the instructions aloud and play the track for students to match the activities in Exercise 2 to the photos.
- Let students compare their answers in pairs before you check them as a class.

ANSWERS / AUDIO SCRIPT 56

1 i 2 f 3 d 4 g 5 a 6 c 7 h 8 j
9 b 10 e

1 I ride my bike all the time. I don't like buses.
2 I meet friends after school. We just sit and talk.
3 One day a week I can play video games. It's usually on Sunday.
4 There's only one plan on Saturday. I go shopping. Shopping's fun!
5 I listen to music all the time. I can't live without music!
6 I sometimes watch television with my family on weekends.
7 Some days I play soccer in the park. There are always people to play with.
8 Some evenings I go on the internet when I finish my homework.
9 When it's a hot day, I sit in the park and read a book.
10 I go to the movies with my friends about one day every month.

Extra activity

In order to draw attention to the time expressions in the recording, hand out copies of the audio script for Exercise 3 and ask students to underline the time expressions. Invite students to share their answers with the class. Then give examples of things you do at those times; for example, *When it's hot, I go to the beach.* Divide the class into pairs and have students tell each other what they do at those times. Encourage students to use the free-time activities from Exercise 2.

4 THE MOVING PICTURE

- Call on a student to read the instructions aloud.
- Play the video for students to watch and write the free-time activities.
- Then play the video again for students to guess which countries the people are in.
- Let students compare their answers in pairs before you check them as a class.

ANSWERS / VIDEO SCRIPT

1 soccer 2 meet friends 3 go shopping 4 ride my bike 5 read a book 6 play video games

1 Brazil 2 USA 3 Italy 4 South Africa 5 Germany 6 Japan

There is no dialog in this video.

WRITE AND SPEAK

5a

- Read the instructions aloud and point out that *top* means *favorite*. For less confident groups, model the activity by writing your top five activities on the board. Remind students to refer to the activities in Exercise 2 and set a time limit of two minutes.

5b

- Read the instructions aloud and ask students to use the useful phrases. Model this stage of the task with more confident students and refer to the notes on the board.
- Divide the class into pairs and set a time limit of three minutes.
- Monitor and note good use of language and errors for feedback at the end of the task.
- Invite students to tell the class about what activities they have in their top five. You could also take a survey to find out the class's overall top five activities.

MOVE BEYOND

Ask students to do the Words & Beyond exercise on page 59.

Homework

Ask students to take a survey of family and friends to find out the most popular free-time activities. Tell them to ask five people they know about each of the activities in Exercise 2. Explain that you'd like students to write sentences about each activity; for example, *Five people go to the movies in their free time; Three people meet friends*; etc. At the beginning of the next class, have students work in small groups to compare their surveys and say which activities are the most popular.

READING We can!

Read an article on a website *Page 42*

STAGE	TIME	FOCUS
GET STARTED		Talk about things you can and can't do.
SPEAK AND READ		Talk about disabilities and read a web article about a deaf boy. Learn how to read the title, headings, and first sentences to help you understand a text (reading subskill).
REACT		Talk about things that are difficult for a deaf person. Think of questions to ask a deaf boy and imagine his answers.

MOVE BEYOND FOR TEACHERS

Talking about disabilities

In recent years, attitudes toward disability have changed a lot. The inclusion of disabled people in schools and communities provides opportunities to learn about diversity and respect for others, as well as academic benefits through collaborative learning. Given the benefits, it is important to talk about disabilities in order to remove any prejudices that may be a barrier to building relationships with disabled people. The topic should be addressed in an uncomplicated way, avoiding inappropriate language and emphasizing the positive (i.e., what disabled people *can* do).

Get started

Set up the topic of the lesson (abilities and disabilities) by writing *I can …* and *I can't …* on the board and telling students some things you can and can't do. Ask students to think of three things they can do and three things they can't do. Then ask students to stand up and talk to different classmates about their ideas and to make a note of people with the same ideas. Set a time limit of three minutes for this task, and then invite students to share what they found out with the class.

SPEAK AND READ

1

- Read the instructions aloud and explain that *disabilities* are the physical or mental conditions that make it difficult for a person to do some things. Point out that the words in the box are disabilities.
- Divide the class into pairs, and then ask students to look at the pictures and match them to the words in the box.
- These are new words, so circulate and help students by encouraging them to think about the words that they know and that can give them a clue to the meaning (e.g., *wheelchair* contains the word *chair*).
- Check answers as a class and drill pronunciation.

ANSWERS
1 deaf 2 blind 3 in a wheelchair

2

- Explain that students are going to read a website article. Call on a student to read the **Reading Tip** aloud, and check understanding of *title* and *headings* by asking students to find them in the article.
- Ask students to read the title, headings, and first sentences. Elicit that this is a website about children with disabilities and the things they can do, and then refer them to the questions.
- Ask students to look quickly at the article and answer the questions.
- Let students compare their answers in pairs before you check them as a class.

ANSWERS
1 His name is Jason Collins.
2 He's from Miami, in the USA.
3 He's deaf.

3 57

- Read the instructions aloud and point out that students have to complete the sentences with two words. Tell students that there are new words in the article and reassure them that you're going to look at them.
- Don't play the audio at this point. It is an extra feature, and a suggestion for using it in class is included at the end of the lesson.
- Set a time limit of three minutes for students to read the article and complete the sentences.
- Let students compare their answers in pairs before you check them as a class.

ANSWERS
1 right ear 2 hearing aid 3 normal things 4 very popular
5 deaf person 6 sign language

Fast finishers
Ask fast finishers to match the questions in the interview to the sentences in Exercise 3.

ANSWERS
How much can you hear? 1, 2
What's it like for a deaf boy at school? 3
You write a very popular blog. Why is it popular? 5
Can other students understand you? 6

4a

- Read the instructions aloud and explain that students have to find phrases in the text to match the sign language in the pictures.
- Let students compare their answers in pairs before you check them as a class.

ANSWERS
He's saying "Hi" (picture 1), "How are you?" (picture 2), and "I'm fine" (picture 3).

4b

- Ask students to practice the sign language. Model the first sign as a whole class.
- Divide the class into pairs for students to practice. Then invite students to do the signs for the class.

Extra activity
Ask students to think of signs for *thanks*, *you're welcome*, *sorry*, *goodbye*. Divide the class into pairs and give students a couple of minutes to prepare. Then have pairs work with another pair and ask them to show their signs for the other pair to guess the phrase. Finally, show students what the real sign language is and ask them how similar their signs are. You can find the correct signs online, for example at http://www.nidcd.nih.gov/health/hearing/pages/asl.aspx#4 or http://www.handspeak.com/word/ or on YouTube.

REACT

5

- Call on students to read the instructions and the question aloud. Then refer students to the useful phrases in the PHRASE BYTES box. Elicit some possible endings for the phrases.
- Give students a minute to think about their answers, and then divide the class into pairs to ask and answer the questions.
- Invite students to share their ideas with the class.

MOVE BEYOND

Ask a student to read the instructions aloud. Explain that students are going to write questions and answers like the ones in the interview.

Divide the class into pairs and set a time limit of three minutes for students to write their questions and answers. Circulate and help where necessary.

After three minutes, stop the activity and have each pairwork with another pair to compare their ideas before sharing them with the class.

Recorded reading text 57
Rather than having students read the website article, ask them to cover the article and play the track for them to complete the sentences in Exercise 3. Then let them compare their answers in pairs before playing the track again for them to check their ideas. Finally, ask students to check their answers with the text before calling on students to share their answers with the class.

Homework

Ask students to think about some of the difficulties a blind person and a person in a wheelchair might experience, and to write three sentences for each. Encourage them to use the useful phrases in the PHRASE BYTES box. At the beginning of the next class, have students work in small groups to compare their ideas.

GRAMMAR *Can/can't*

Talk about the things you can do

Page 43

STAGE	TIME	FOCUS
GET STARTED		Review free-time activities.
READ AND LISTEN		Read and listen to a conversation about a girl's disability.
STUDY		Use the text to help you complete examples with *can* and *can't*.
PRACTICE		Practice using *can/can't* in controlled exercises.
SPEAK		Talk about things you can and can't do.

Get started

In order to review and consolidate free-time activities from pages 40–41 and learn new vocabulary that students will use later in this lesson, write the verbs *read*, *listen*, *play*, *speak*, and *touch* in circles on the board and elicit some words that collocate with them. Write the collocations on the board and connect them to the appropriate circle with a line.

Divide the class into pairs and set a time limit of two minutes for students to brainstorm as many collocations as possible for each of the words. After two minutes, stop the activity and have students work with another pair to share their lists and teach each other new words. Circulate while they are doing this to check collocations and spelling.

READ AND LISTEN Grammar in context

1 58

- Ask students to look at the picture and say what they can see (*two girls talking and eating lunch*).
- Read the instructions aloud, and then play the track for students to listen and read the text.
- Let them compare their answer in pairs before you check it as a class.

ANSWER / AUDIO SCRIPT 58

She's blind.

See Student's Book, page 45, for audio script.

STUDY

2

- Elicit that we use *can/can't* to talk about abilities. Refer students to the table and ask them to complete the examples with *can* and *can't*.
- Ask students to look at the conversation in Exercise 1 to check the answers that are in the conversation. Then check answers as a class.
- Point out that *can/can't* do not change their form.
- Refer students to the **Grammar Database** on page 55.

ANSWERS

can can't see Can can't

PRACTICE

3

- Read the instructions aloud and refer students to the example. Remind students that Maya is the blind girl in the conversation in Exercise 1.
- Ask students to choose the correct options to complete the sentences.
- Let them compare their answers in pairs before you check them as a class.

ANSWERS

2 can't 3 can't 4 can 5 can't

4a

- Read the instructions aloud. Ask students to look at the photo of Mateo and elicit some ideas of things he can and can't do.
- Refer students to the prompts and set a time limit of three minutes for them to write sentences.
- Let students compare their answers in pairs, but don't check them at this stage.

4b 59

- Play the track for students to listen and check their answers. Then call on students to share their answers with the class.

ANSWERS / AUDIO SCRIPT 59

1 He can swim.
2 He can't walk.
3 He can take the bus.
4 He can't ride a bike.
5 He can't play soccer.
6 He can play basketball.

1 I can swim.
2 I can't walk.
3 I can take the bus.
4 I can't ride a bike.
5 I can't play soccer.
6 I can play basketball.

5a

- Read the instructions aloud and go over the example.
- Set a time limit of three minutes for students to write the questions. Circulate and give help as necessary.
- Let students compare their answers in pairs. Then call on students to share their answers with the class.

ANSWERS
2 Can you say *yes* in German?
3 Can your teacher play tennis?
4 Can people in New Zealand speak English?
5 Can you touch your head with your foot?
6 Can you and your classmates be quiet for 10 minutes?

5b

- Ask students to answer the questions using short answers. Refer them to the example and elicit some answers from the class.
- Set a time limit of two minutes for students to write their answers.
- Let students compare their answers in pairs before you check them as a class.

ANSWERS
2 Yes, I can. / No, I can't.
3 Yes, he/she can. / No, he/she can't.
4 Yes, they can.
5 Yes, I can. / No, I can't.
6 Yes, we can. / No, we can't.

Fast finishers
Ask fast finishers to look back at the interview on page 42 and underline all the uses of *can/can't*.

SPEAK

6

- Read the instructions aloud and refer students to the examples. Model some questions with more confident students in the class.
- Divide the class into groups of three and set a time limit of three minutes for the activity. Circulate and give help as necessary.
- Stop the activity after three minutes and ask several students to tell you what they found out in their groups.

Alternative procedure: less confident classes
Before doing the activity in Exercise 6, have students brainstorm ideas for questions. Set a time limit of two minutes, and then invite students to share their ideas with the class. Write the verbs they mention on the board and suggest that they refer to them during Exercise 6.

Homework

Ask students to continue the conversation between Jan and Maya. Explain that Jan has a lot of questions to ask Maya and that students should write three more questions and Maya's answers. Ask students to use questions with *can* and to include *can/can't* in the answers. At the beginning of the next class, have students work in small groups to compare their conversations. Ask several students to share some of the questions they wrote.

LISTENING AND VOCABULARY Are you musical?

Listen to street interviews *Page 46*

STAGE	TIME	FOCUS
GET STARTED		Play a game to practice *can/can't* for abilities.
WORK WITH WORDS		Learn and practice using words for musical instruments and types of music.
LISTEN		Listen to street interviews and identify people's musical talents (listening subskill).
REACT		Talk about whether you're musical.

Get started

Play *20 questions* to practice *can/can't*. Ask students to think of superheroes (e.g., *Superman, Wolverine, Catwoman*, etc.) and their special abilities. As students may lack the vocabulary for this, elicit a number of useful verbs and write them on the board (e.g., *fly, swim, climb buildings, see through walls*, etc.). Ask one student to think of a superhero. The rest of the class can ask 20 questions, but the students can answer only *yes* or *no*. After 20 questions the class has to take a guess. Encourage students to use questions and short answers with *can*.

WORK WITH WORDS Music

1 60

- Ask students to look at the pictures and match them to the instruments in the box. Set a time limit of two minutes.
- Play the track for students to listen and check their answers.
- Continue the track for students to listen and repeat the words.

ANSWERS / AUDIO SCRIPT 60
drums 2 guitar 5 keyboard 1 piano 4 violin 3
drums guitar keyboard piano violin

2a 61

- Divide the class into pairs and ask students to listen to the music and match each piece to a type of music in the box.
- Play the track for students to listen and decide what type of music each piece is. There is no audio script because the track has examples of music, but no conversation. Answers are in Exercise 2b.

2b 62

- Play the track for students to listen and check their answers.
- Continue the track for students to listen and repeat the words.

ANSWERS / AUDIO SCRIPT 62

classical 2 hip-hop 5 Latin 4 pop 1 rock 3

classical hip-hop Latin pop rock

3a 63 PRONOUNCE

- Play the track for students to listen and repeat the /v/ sound. Model the sound for students to copy and practice.

AUDIO SCRIPT 63

violin

3b 64

- Play the track for students to listen and repeat the words.

AUDIO SCRIPT 64

See Student's Book, page 44, for audio script.

Extra activity

To give students extra practice saying the /v/ sound, write the following tongue twisters on the board:

We have a very vibrant piece for violin.

Valiant superheroes fight vicious villains in this movie.

Say the tongue twisters aloud and then give students a minute to practice saying them. Then divide the class into pairs and ask students to practice saying them together.

4

- Explain that students are going to work in pairs and ask and answer questions about music.
- Ask a student to read the questions aloud, and then refer students to the PHRASE BYTES box. Elicit some possible endings for the phrases and ask students to use the phrases in their answers. You may want to model one or two of the questions and answers with a confident student.
- Divide the class into pairs and set a time limit of three minutes for students to ask and answer the questions.
- Stop the activity and invite students to tell the class about their partners.
- Ask students to do the Move Beyond task on page 59.

LISTEN

5 65

- Go over the instructions. Then call on a student to read the question and the names of the people aloud. Check that students understand what a street interview is and remind them to write *yes* or *no* next to each name.
- Play the track for students to listen and decide whether the people are musical or not.
- Let them compare their answers in pairs before you check them as a class.

ANSWERS / AUDIO SCRIPT 65

Dora, yes Penny, no Neil, yes Rianna, yes

1

Dave: Hello! Welcome to *Play It Again*, a television show about music. Today we're asking the question: *Are you musical?*
Dave: Hi there. I'm from *Play It Again*!
Dora: What's that?
Dave: It's a television show. What's your name?
Dora: Dora.
Dave: Are you musical?
Dora: I play the violin, so yes.
Dave: What's your favorite kind of music?
Dora: Classical music.
Dave: Really? What about pop?
Dora: No, it's boring.

2

Dave: Hello! What are your names?
Penny: I'm Penny, and this is Neil.
Dave: Are you musical?
Penny: I'm not. He is. He plays the guitar and keyboard, and he writes songs.
Dave: Really? What kind of songs?
Neil: Pop songs.
Dave: Can you sing a song for us?
Neil: No way!

3

Dave: Excuse me? What's your name?
Rianna: Rianna.
Dave: Are you musical?
Rianna: Not really. I can't play an instrument.
Dave: What's your favorite kind of music?
Rianna: Latin. I go to salsa classes.
Dave: You can dance! So you *are* musical!
Rianna: Yeah. OK. So, I am musical.

6 65

- Read the instructions aloud and give students a minute to read through the sentences.
- Play the track for students to listen and complete the sentences.
- Let them compare their answers in pairs before you check them as a class.

ANSWERS / AUDIO SCRIPT 65

1 Neil 2 Dora 3 Rianna 4 Dora 5 Rianna
6 Dora and Neil

See Exercise 5 for audio script.

Alternative procedure: less confident classes

The audio recording is fairly long, which may be overwhelming for less confident students. There are several ways to help them.

- Pause the track after each speaker to give students thinking time.
- Play the track again after students have compared their answers in pairs and before checking them as a class.
- Give students the audio script to read while listening to the track to check their answers.

REACT

7

- Ask students to look at the question and think about any musical instruments they play, the music they listen to, and the kinds of dances they can do.
- Refer them to the PHRASE BYTES box. Check that students understand the phrases and elicit endings for them.

- Divide the class into small groups and have students ask and answer the question. Set a time limit of two minutes.
- Monitor and note errors and good use of language to go over in a feedback session at the end of the activity.
- Stop the activity and call on students to tell the class about their group's answers. Ask students to decide whether the class is generally musical and to say why or why not.

MOVE BEYOND

Ask students to do the Words & Beyond exercise on page 59.

Homework

Ask students to choose three of the types of music from Exercise 2 and to think of groups that play those types of music. Ask them to find out what musical instruments are in those groups and to make a list in their notebooks. At the beginning of the next class, ask students to work in pairs and tell each other about the groups and their instruments. If possible, encourage students to play each other some samples of their chosen music.

GRAMMAR Simple present

Talk about habits and routines *Page 45*

STAGE	TIME	FOCUS
GET STARTED		Play a game to review music vocabulary.
READ AND LISTEN		Read and listen to an interview with a pop group.
STUDY		Use the text to help you complete examples with the simple present.
PRACTICE		Learn endings for third person singular verbs. Practice using the simple present in controlled exercises.
WRITE AND SPEAK		Write and talk about a famous group or singer.

Get started

To review music vocabulary and practice using *can/can't*, play a game of *Find Someone Who …* (see Games, page 29). Prepare a worksheet with *Find Someone Who …* and the phrases *can play the piano*, *can't play a musical instrument*, *listens to hip-hop*, *can dance salsa*, *can play the drums*, and *plays in a group*. Make sure students understand the activity and set a time limit of three minutes for them to walk around and try to find people for each of the statements. Monitor and note errors and good use of language to go over in a feedback session at the end of the activity.

READ AND LISTEN Grammar in context

1 66

- Ask students to look at the picture and say what instruments they can see (*guitar and violin*).
- Read the instructions aloud. Then play the track and check the answer as a class.

ANSWER / AUDIO SCRIPT 66

They're from the same family / are brother and sisters.

See Student's Book, page 45, for audio script.

Alternative procedure: more confident classes

Have students close their books and listen to the track to answer the question. Then ask them to open their books and check their answer with the text.

Extra activity

Ask students to read the interview again and label the people in the picture.

ANSWERS

(Left to right) Jackie's sister, Jackie's brother (Max), Jackie (speaker)

STUDY

2

- Refer students to the table and ask them to complete it with words from the interview.
- Let them compare their answers in pairs before you check them as a class. Point out that the simple present form changes in the third person singular. Write these verbs on the board: *play, do, watch, cry.* Go over the spelling of the third person singular form of each verb. Explain the rules, pointing out that *-y* changes to *-ies* only after a consonant. Elicit other examples (e.g., *like, go, miss, try*).
- Refer students to the **Grammar Database** on page 55. Highlight the issues of pronunciation. (See Teaching Tips, *The /iz/ sound*, page 28.)

ANSWERS

play plays goes teaches has

PRACTICE

3

- Explain that in the exercise students practice the third person singular forms.
- Ask students to write the third person singular forms of the verbs by adding *-s*, *-es*, or *-ies*.
- Let them compare their answers in pairs before you check them as a class.

ANSWERS
2 watches 3 reads 4 talks 5 practices
6 does 7 studies 8 arrives

4

- Explain that students are going to read about another group, The Lateens, and read the instructions aloud. Remind students to use the verbs from Exercise 3.
- Set a time limit of three minutes for students to complete the text with the verbs in Exercise 3.
- Let them compare their answers in pairs before you check them as a class.

ANSWERS
2 talks 3 listens 4 studies 5 arrives
6 practices 7 does 8 watches

Fast finishers
Ask fast finishers to underline all the time expressions in the description.

5

- Ask students to look at the message from The Lateens on their website and to complete it with the simple present form of the verbs in parentheses.
- Set a time limit of three minutes for the task.
- Let students compare their answers in pairs before you check them as a class.

ANSWERS
2 play 3 come 4 teaches 5 plays 6 copies
7 has 8 invite

WRITE AND SPEAK

6a

- Ask a student to read the instructions aloud. Then divide the class into pairs.
- Set a time limit of three minutes for students to write their sentences. Ask them to refer to the **Grammar Database** on page 55 and the texts in Exercises 4 and 5.
- Circulate and give help as necessary.

6b

- Read the instructions aloud and point out that the pairs should take turns talking about their group or singer for the other pair to guess who it is.
- Give students a moment to read their sentences and think about what they're going to say. Then have students work with another pair to do the task.
- Invite students to tell the class about the groups or singers they talked about.

Homework

Ask students to research a pop group and to write a description (about 60 words) similar to the one in Exercise 5. Ask them to write about where they are from, the music they play, and their instruments, but not to write the name of the band. At the beginning of the next class, have students display their descriptions around the classroom and give them a few minutes to read different descriptions and guess who the groups are.

LANGUAGE & BEYOND *SCHOOL SKILLS*

Write down your homework *Page 46*

STAGE	TIME	FOCUS
GET STARTED		Review classroom vocabulary.
SPEAK AND READ		Read and talk about how teachers give homework and how students write it down.
DO		Look at two homework planners. Answer questions about the homework planners and say which planner has more information.
REFLECT		Talk about homework.
EXTEND		Write down your English homework in English.

SCHOOL SKILLS

WRITE DOWN YOUR HOMEWORK
Most teachers like to give some homework, either to check understanding of new information or to give students the chance to develop skills such as writing or reading. However, as most teachers know, students don't always do the homework, often because it hasn't been written down properly. It is therefore important that a routine for assigning homework be established and that students know what's expected of them. In this lesson, students discuss ways that homework is assigned and the way they write it down. It is also a good opportunity for teachers to clarify what's expected and to think about how they assign homework. Ask yourself *Are the instructions clear? Are they written clearly on the board? How do I want students to do homework? Do I want parents to be involved in checking that their children are doing the homework?*

Get started

To prepare students for the lesson, review classroom vocabulary. Divide the class into pairs and ask them to brainstorm things, furniture, and people in the classroom. Set a time limit of three minutes, and then invite students to come to the board and write their words. Then ask students to make three columns in their notebooks with the headings *things*, *furniture*, and *people*, and ask them to write the classroom words in the correct columns. Check answers as a class, and then have students "test" each other: without looking at their lists, one student says a word and the other says the category.

SPEAK AND READ

1

- Read the instructions aloud and ask students to choose the options that are correct for them.
- Divide the class into pairs and ask students to compare their answers.
- Call on students to share their ideas with the class and ask the class whether they agree or disagree.

2a

- Read the instructions aloud and call on students to read the lists aloud.
- Refer students to the picture and elicit some of the things they can see.
- Ask students to check the things in the lists they can see in the picture.
- Let them compare their answers in pairs before you check them as a class.

ANSWERS

How teachers can give homework:
Write it on the board. ✓
How students can write down homework:
Make a note on a phone. ✓
Write it on a piece of paper. ✓
Write it in a homework plannerr. ✓

2b

- Read the instructions and the questions aloud, and then refer students to the PHRASE BYTES box.
- Divide the class into pairs and ask students to discuss the questions.
- Invite students to share their ideas with the class.

DO

3

- Read the instructions aloud and refer students to the two homework planners. Divide the class into pairs to discuss the questions.
- Call on students to share their answers with the class.

ANSWERS

1 a both b 2 c 2 d 1
2 Planner 2 has more information.

Extra activity
Ask students to look at the last entry in their homework planners and answer questions a–d. Then have them compare their answers in groups and say whether it's a good way to write down their homework.

REFLECT

4

- Read the questions aloud and refer students to the PHRASE BYTES box. Make sure students understand the expressions and encourage them to use them in their answers.
- Divide the class into small groups and set a time limit of three minutes for students to discuss the questions.
- Ask a student to read the REFLECTION POINT aloud and check that they understand *task*. Then ask students if they agree with the advice and to give their reasons.

EXTEND

5

- Read the instructions aloud and then assign students some homework! Write the homework clearly on the board and ask students to write it down.
- Circulate and check that students are making a clear note of their homework, and refer them to planner 2 if necessary.

Homework

Ask students to design a web page with tips on how to do homework. Explain that they should say how to write down homework, as well as where and when to do homework. In order to prepare for the task, brainstorm ideas as a class. Remind students to use the imperative and encourage them to illustrate their tips with pictures. At the beginning of the next class, ask students to work in small groups to compare their web pages and decide which they like the best.

SPEAKING What time is it?

Tell the time

Page 49

STAGE	TIME	FOCUS
GET STARTED		Review telling the time in English.
SPEAK		Look at a picture and say what you can see.
LISTEN		Listen to four conversations and write the times they mention. Practice asking for and telling the time (speaking subskill).
ACT		Write and act out different conversations where you ask for and tell the time.

MOVE BEYOND FOR TEACHERS

Telling the time

There are different ways of telling the time in English. In this lesson, students learn how to say the minutes (or *a quarter past/ to*; *half past*) before the hour (e.g., *twenty-five past six*, *a quarter to seven*, etc.). Another way is by saying the hour before the minutes, (e.g., *six twenty-five*, *six forty-five*). The former is more difficult to learn but worth practicing, as it is commonly used. One way to ensure that students get regular practice telling the time is to ask them the time at certain points in each class, or when you see them looking at their watches.

Get started

Find out how well students can tell the time by drawing different clocks (both analog and digital) and times on the board. Divide the class into pairs and ask students to say the times. Circulate and give help as necessary. If students find the task difficult, encourage them to use the simpler structure of hour before minutes. Call on students to say the times for the class and drill the times chorally.

SPEAK

1

- Read the instructions aloud and refer students to the PHRASE BYTES box. Model some ways of using the expressions (e.g., *In this picture, there's a sidewalk*).
- Divide the class into pairs and have students answer the questions, but don't check the answers at this stage.

LISTEN

2 67

- Ask students to listen to the conversations and check their answer to Exercise 1.
- Call on students to share their answers to the questions in Exercises 1 and 2 with the class, and ask students how Mike feels (*nervous*).

ANSWERS / AUDIO SCRIPT 67

Mike and Kelly are at a bus stop because they want to go to a movie. At the end, they decide to go home.

1
Mike: What time is the movie?
Kelly: It's at seven o'clock.
Mike: What time is it now?
Kelly: It's a quarter after six.
Mike: We have time.

2
Mike: Kelly? What time is it?
Kelly: It's six thirty.
Mike: It's six thirty? The bus is late!

3
Mike: Kelly? What time is it now?
Kelly: It's six thirty-five.
Mike: Twenty-five to seven! Oh no! Where's the bus?

4
Mike: Kelly? What time is it?
Kelly: It's a quarter to seven. Let's go home.
Mike: Good idea.

3

- Read the instructions aloud and go over the example.
- Ask students to write the times under the clocks.
- Let students compare their answers in pairs before you check them as a class. Elicit the stressed words and syllables (e.g., *seven o'clock*, *a quarter after six*, *six thirty*). Model and do a choral drill of the times.

ANSWERS

2 a quarter after / past six / six fifteen
3 six thirty / half past six
4 six thirty-five / twenty-five to seven
5 six forty-five / a quarter to seven

4 68

- Ask students to underline the questions for asking about the time in Exercise 2 and check as a class.
- Read the instructions aloud, and then play the track for students to listen and repeat the questions and times.

AUDIO SCRIPT 68

1
Mike: What time is the movie?
Kelly: It's at seven o'clock.

2
Mike: What time is it now?
Kelly: It's a quarter after six.

3
Mike: What time is it?
Kelly: It's six thirty.

4
Mike: Twenty-five to seven?

5
Mike: What time is it?
Kelly: It's a quarter to seven.

5a

- Read the instructions aloud and refer students to the clock. Remind them that *after* and *past* both mean *past* the hour and *to* means *before*.
- Invite a confident student to come to the board and draw the first clock. Then give students three minutes to draw the other clocks.
- Circulate and check that students are drawing the correct times.
- Stop the activity and invite students to come to the board to draw the clocks.

ANSWERS

Fast finishers

Ask fast finishers to draw more clocks and write the times on a separate piece of paper. Students can then use these clocks for the activity in Exercise 5b.

5b

- Go over the instructions and refer students to the PHRASEBOOK. Play the track for them to listen and repeat the questions and times.
- Divide the class into pairs and set a time limit of three minutes for students to point to the clocks they drew in Exercise 5a and ask for the time.
- Circulate and give help as necessary.

ACT

6 69

- Call on students to read the instructions aloud. Remind them to use the PHRASEBOOK to help them.
- Divide the class into pairs and set a time limit of five minutes for students to write their conversations. Circulate and give help as necessary.
- Give students five minutes to practice their conversations. Then ask the pairs to act out their conversations for another pair. Explain that the pair that is listening should write down the times they hear and then say what the situation is.

Homework

Ask students to think of five times in the day that are important for them (e.g., *seven thirty – get up*, *one o'clock – have lunch*, etc.) and to draw clocks for those times. At the beginning of the next class, have students work in pairs to show each other their clocks and guess why the times are important; for example, *I think you get up at seven o'clock. Yes, that's right.*

WRITING My free time

Write an email Page 48

STAGE	TIME	FOCUS
GET STARTED		Play a game to practice simple present verbs and review free-time activities from the unit.
SPEAK AND READ		Discuss survey questions. Read an email and learn how to use capital letters (writing subskill).
PRACTICE		Practice using capital letters by rewriting an email.
DISCUSS		Talk about your free-time activities.
WRITE		Write an email to a pen pal about your free-time activities.
SHARE		Compare your email with other students' emails to find people with similar free-time activities.

Get started

Play a game of *True or False?* to practice using the simple present and to review language from the unit. Ask students to write sentences using the simple present and free-time activities from the unit on a piece of paper. Some of their sentences should be true and some false. Then have them trade sentences with a partner, read them, and guess whether they are true or false. To make the game more communicative, encourage students to ask each other questions to help them decide.

SPEAK AND READ

1

- Read the instructions aloud and give students a minute to complete the survey.
- Refer them to the useful expressions in the PHRASE BYTES box, and then divide the class into pairs and ask students to compare their answers.
- Invite students to share their answers with the class and find out how many students use email and what they use it for.

MOVE BEYOND FOR TEACHERS

Pen pals

A pen pal is a person to whom you write letters or emails and who is usually in another country. Pen pals are a good way to practice other languages and learn about other cultures.

2

- Ask students to read the email and answer the question.
- Let them compare their answers in pairs before you check the answer as a class.

ANSWER
Clara is Greta's new pen pal in Argentina.

Extra activity
Check students' comprehension of Greta's email by writing the following sentences on the board and asking students to correct them.

1 *Greta is from Argentina.*
2 *Greta speaks Spanish.*
3 *Greta's sister has guitar classes.*
4 *Greta plays in a group.*

ANSWERS
1 Clara is from Argentina.
2 Greta speaks English. / Greta doesn't speak Spanish. / Clara speaks Spanish.
3 Greta has guitar classes.
4 Greta's sister plays in a group.

3

- Ask a student to read the tips from the HOW TO box aloud. As the rules for capitalization are often different in other languages, you could ask students about similarities and differences with their language; for example, in Spanish, languages and days of the week don't have capital letters, but the beginning of a new sentence does.
- Ask students to look at the email again and circle other examples of capital letters. You could also ask students to say which rule they correspond to (*starting a sentence, a language, a name*, etc.).
- Check answers as a class.

ANSWER
Hi Clara,
It's great to have a new pen pal in Argentina. I can't speak Spanish, so we can practice our English. You ask about my free time. Well, I meet my friends, go shopping, and go on the internet. On Mondays I have a guitar class. My sister teaches me too. She plays in a group.
Write soon,
Greta

PRACTICE

4

- Read the instructions aloud and elicit a couple of examples from the class.
- Set a time limit of three minutes for students to rewrite the email with capital letters.
- Let them compare their answers in pairs before you check them as a class.

ANSWER
Hi Greta,
Thanks for your email. It's great to have a pen pal in Germany. Is German difficult? I think I'm a typical teenager. I meet my friends in my free time too. On Saturdays we go to the movies. At home I listen to music, but I can't play an instrument.
Best wishes,
Clara

Fast finishers
As fast finishers may have rushed through the exercise and missed some of the examples, tell them how many capitals they should have (17) and ask them to check their answer to make sure they have all of them.

DISCUSS

5

- Explain that students are going to write an email to a pen pal about their free-time activities. Direct their attention to the questions and explain that the questions can help them think about what to write.
- Divide the class into pairs and give them several minutes to tell each other about their free-time activities and things they can do.

WRITE

6

- Refer students to the three points about writing the email and check that they understand each point. Give them a few minutes to think about what they want to write.
- Set a time limit of 10 minutes for students to write their emails. Remind them to look back at the tips in the HOW TO box for help. Circulate and give help as necessary.
- When students have finished writing, ask them to check their emails against the three points to make sure they have followed all of the instructions.

SHARE

7

- Divide the class into small groups. Ask students to read their emails aloud. Tell them to make a list of activities that most people in their group have in common and another list of activities that only one person in the group does.
- When they have finished, ask the groups to tell the class what activities most people in the group have in common and then to say whether there were any activities that only one person does.

Homework

Ask students to write an email to you telling you about their English class. Write some prompts on the board and have students copy them in their notebooks: *What activities do you like? What can you do well? What can't you do very well? What topics do you want to learn about?* Check that students understand the questions and ask them to answer them in their email. Encourage them to write 50–60 words. At the beginning of the next class, have students compare their emails in groups. Then have a class discussion about each question. You can use this information to help you adapt the course to suit the needs of your students.

VOCABULARY Free-time activities

1

- Refer students to the text and explain that it is an ad for a club where you can go in your free time. Ask them if they know any similar clubs.
- Ask students to complete the ad with the words in the box.
- Let students compare their answers in pairs before you check them as a class.

ANSWERS
1 a book 2 the internet 3 soccer 4 my bike
5 friends 6 television 7 video games 8 music
9 the movies 10 shopping

Music

2

- Ask students to complete the words for instruments and types of music you can learn at the club. Point out that some of the letters of each word are given and that there is one blank for each letter.
- Let students compare their answers in pairs before you check them as a class.

ANSWERS
1 drums 2 guitar 3 keyboard 4 piano 5 violin
6 classical 7 hip-hop 8 Latin 9 pop 10 rock

GRAMMAR *Can/can't*

3

- Explain that students are going to read a conversation about the TLC club.
- Ask students to read the conversation quickly first. Then ask them to complete the conversation using *can/can't* and the words in parentheses where necessary.
- Let students compare their answers in pairs before you check them as a class.

ANSWERS
1 Can I study 2 can 3 can play 4 Can you play
5 can't 6 Can she teach 7 can't come 8 can be

Simple present

4

- Explain that the email is about classes at the club.
- Ask students to read the email quickly first. Then ask them to complete it with the simple present form of the verbs in parentheses.
- Let students compare their answers in pairs before you check them as a class.

ANSWERS
1 go 2 comes 3 studies 4 teaches 5 have
6 finishes 7 want

SKILLS CHECK

- Ask students to think about what they've learned in this unit and to check the sentences.
- Divide the class into pairs to discuss what they've learned, and use this as an opportunity to review anything students still have difficulties with.

Extra Resources

Go to the Teacher's Resource Center at mee2.macmillaneducation.com for:

- downloadable audio and audio scripts for the Student's Book and Workbook
- videos, video worksheets, and video scripts
- extra vocabulary at two levels of difficulty
- extra grammar at two levels of difficulty
- CLIL lessons, with full teacher's notes
- school skills lessons, with full teacher's notes
- Speaking Database materials
- the *Move Beyond Intro A Level* wordlist
- downloadable PDF and Word tests for Unit 4 (all skills)
- the *Move Beyond Intro A Level* Midterm Test (all skills)
- tips for using the Grammar Database
- extra reading materials
- and more!

Go to the Workbook pages 106–117 for further practice material.

PROGRESS CHECK UNITS 3&4

Preparing for the Progress Check

Vocabulary review

- Divide the class into four teams (call them A, B, C, and D) and give each team a category from the following: *Pet animals, Things in your room, Free-time activities,* and *Music.* Ask students to find their category in the Unit Reviews (pages 39 and 49).
- Ask the teams to come up with clues for six of the words in their category; for example, *You can tell the time with this.* (*clock*) or *This animal lives in water* (*fish*). One member of the team should write down the clues.
- Once the teams have written six clues, ask Team A to read their clues aloud. The first person on another team to guess each word correctly wins a point for that team. Keep score on the board.
- When Team A has read all their clues aloud, have the other teams take turns reading their clues. The team with the most points at the end is the winner.

Grammar review

- Ask students to look back through Units 3 and 4. Ask them to raise their hands when they find a grammar point they've studied in these units. Ask the first student who raised a hand to write the grammar heading on the board.
- Repeat with three more students until you have the following on the board: (Unit 3) Imperatives and object pronouns; *There is / there are*; (Unit 4) *Can/can't;* Simple present.
- Ask the following questions about the grammar points:
  When do we use imperatives? (to give orders and instructions)
  When do we use object pronouns? (as the object of a verb or after prepositions)
  When do we use there is *or* there are? *(to say that something exists)*
  When do we use can/can't? *(to talk about abilities)*
  When do we use the simple present? (to talk about habits and routines)
- Divide the class into pairs and encourage students to write examples for each grammar point. Walk around, monitoring and helping if necessary.

Optional warm-up activities

READ Exercise 1

- Ask students to look at Exercise 1 in the Progress Check and ask the following questions: *How many sentences are there?* (*six, including the example sentence*); *What kind of questions are they?* (*multiple-choice questions*); *How many answer choices are there?* (*three*).
- Refer students to the sentences and ask them to say in which sentences:
  there are verbs for answer choices (*0, 5*)
  there are activities for answer choices (*1, 4*)
  there are prepositions for answer choices (*2, 3*)
- Going through the example together should help students gain confidence to attempt the rest on their own. If they find it difficult, encourage students to discuss the first question with a partner.

LISTEN Exercise 2

- Refer students to Exercise 2 and elicit useful information about the listening task by discussing the following questions.
  Who is talking? (*Delia and Luke*)
  What are they talking about? (*what animals and pets the people in Delia's family have*)
  How many people in Delia's family do they talk about? (*six*)
- Divide the class into pairs or small groups and ask them to discuss which animals or pets they think each family member has. After two or three minutes, ask students around the class to say what pet they think one of the people has and to explain their choice.

WRITE Exercise 3

- Refer students back to some fill-in-the-blank exercises they've done recently (e.g., Exercises 4 and 5, page 47), and remind them that they can usually predict the kind of word that is needed in each blank (*verb, preposition, object pronoun*, etc.).
- Divide the class into pairs or small groups and ask them to look carefully at Exercise 3 and figure out what kind of word is needed in each blank.
- Write 1–10 on the board, and for each blank ask students to tell you what kind of word they need to write in it.

Doing the Progress Check

READ Exercise 1

- If you've decided not to do the full warm-up, focus students' attention on the picture in Exercise 1 in the Progress Check and ask *What's Oliver's free-time activity? What other free-time activities can you remember?*
- Draw students' attention to the example and ask them to say why the answer is C (*we use* watch *when we look at something carefully, usually something moving. The television doesn't move, but we watch the moving images carefully*) and can't be the other two options (*Option A – we use* look *for the moment when we direct our attention to something and Option B – we use* see *when we look at things we don't intend to look at but that just happen to be there*).
- Go through the **Test-Taking Tips** with the class and make sure they understand how to complete sentences with multiple-choice answers.
- Allow 10 minutes for this section.

ANSWERS
1 A 2 C 3 B 4 B 5 C

LISTEN Exercise 2

▶70

- If you have decided not to do the full warm-up, ask students to say the names of the pets in the photos in Exercise 2. Make sure they know what the other animals and pets in the list are. Encourage students to speculate on which animal or pet each person in Delia's family has.
- Go through the **Test-Taking Tips** and make sure students understand that they have to write a letter next to each person. Remind them that they don't need to use all the letters.
- Point out that they will hear everything twice.
- Allow 10 minutes for this section.

ANSWERS/ AUDIO SCRIPT ▶70

1 F 2 E 3 G 4 A 5 C

Luke: I really want a dog. Does your family have any pets, Delia?
Delia: Yes, they do. Mom has a cat – but it's a bad cat. Dad has some fish. The cat likes Dad's fish and tries to eat them. So the cat isn't Dad's favorite animal.
Luke: What about your brother?
Delia: The cat isn't my brother's favorite animal either! He has a mouse – a white one.
Luke: A mouse? Ugh!
Delia: I like the mouse. But the cat likes the mouse too!
Luke: Oh no. Does your sister have a pet?
Delia: Well, it's not really a pet. She loves horses, so she has a horse. It's black, and its name is Bob.
Luke: Wow! A horse. That's cool.
Delia: My grandmother and grandfather have animals too.
Luke: What do they have?
Delia: Well, Grandma has a little bird, and Grandpa has chickens. I feed them when I visit Grandma and Grandpa.
Luke: You're so lucky!

WRITE Exercise 3

- If you have decided not to do the full warm-up, briefly refer students back to the writing exercises and task on page 48. Ask them what they learned from these tasks.
- Go through the **Test-Taking Tips** for the writing task and draw students' attention to the example. Remind students to read carefully because their answers must fit logically in the sentence.
- Explain that spelling is important for this task, and on a real test they would lose credit for spelling mistakes.
- Allow 10 to 15 minutes for this section.

ANSWERS

1 do 2 ride 3 go 4 a 5 her 6 after/past / to
7 can't 8 can 9 have 10 Write

After the Progress Check

Optional game

Play a game of *Broken Telephone* (see Games, page 29). This game will help lighten the atmosphere after the Progress Check, and it follows up on the different vocabulary and grammar covered in it.

Ask students to memorize and pass on these sentences.

Grandpa has five chickens, and my brother has a black horse.
My cat is old and a little deaf, but she's very smart.
I have a guitar class on Monday with a teacher from Argentina.
I can't play an instrument, but I can ride a bike.
I'm crazy about music, and I play in a group.

Feedback and extension

After the Progress Check has been graded, provide feedback to the class as a whole and individually as far as possible. Ask students which parts they found the most difficult and how they think they could improve their grades next time.

READ Exercise 1

- Review the sentences one at a time and encourage students to say why the other options are wrong. Where there were mistakes, find out whether the problems were in understanding the sentences or the options.
- Encourage students to read in English as much as they can. Remind students that a lot of online material they see will be in English, although not all of this is written in good English.

LISTEN Exercise 2

- Handing out photocopies of the audio script is a good way to provide feedback. Deal with any mistakes in this way. Seeing the conversation written down helps students recognize when they have misheard something. It will also help them become aware of distractors.

WRITE Exercise 3

- Point out where students lost credit and ask them to review these areas:
  Simple present 1, 2, 3, 9
  Article 4
  Object pronoun 5
  Time 6
  can/can't 7, 8
  Starting and finishing emails 10
- To give further practice with this type of task, ask students to make a similar text with blanks. Divide the class into A/B pairs. Refer Student As to the text in Exercise 2, page 48, and Student Bs to the text in Exercise 1, page 45. Ask students to write out the texts with 10 blanks for the different grammar points covered in Units 3 and 4. Then have students switch texts to test each other. When students create their own tests, they become more aware of the test format and how it tests reading ability and vocabulary knowledge.

WORKBOOK AUDIO SCRIPT

Track ▶71

Starter, page 68, Exercise 3a

1 I'm 18.
2 She's 12.
3 I'm 30.
4 He's 40.
5 I'm 19.
6 Mary's 17.
7 I'm 60.
8 John's five.

Track ▶72

Unit 1, page 74, Exercise 2 and Exercise 3

Italian: Italy is famous for sports cars like the Ferrari. Italians also design beautiful clothes. And they love food too. Like lasagna and risotto – mmm!
Brazilian: Brazilian dance and music are famous. Food from Brazil goes to other countries. They produce coffee and bananas.
German: They're good at technology in Germany. Germans make cars and laptops.
Japanese: Japan has famous clothes designers, and Japanese cars and computers are all over the world.

Track ▶73

Unit 1, page 74, Exercise 5 and Exercise 7

Lin: I like your T-shirt. Where's it from?
Avra: It's from my vacation in Turkey.
Lin: But the words on it are in English, not Turkish. What's on the label?
Avra: I don't know. Wait a minute ... It says, "Made in China." It's Chinese.
Lin: Oh.

Track ▶74

Unit 1, page 77, Exercise 1b

Ask for a description of something
What color is it?
What's your house like?
Is it big?
Is it small?
Describe something
It's black.
It's red.
They are Italian.
They are Brazilian.
They're very nice.
They're really nice.
The neighbors are noisy.
The neighbors are quiet.

Track ▶75

Unit 1, page 77, Exercise 2 and Exercise 3

Conversation 1
Diego: Where are you from, Lara?
Lara: I'm from Rio – I'm Brazilian.
Diego: What's it like there?
Lara: Rio is a very big city. Where are *you* from, Diego?
Diego: I'm Colombian – from the capital city, Bogotá. It's a big city too.
Conversation 2
Mina: Nice party, Zac.
Zac: What?
Mina: Nice party.
Zac: It's very noisy.
Mina: But it's a lot of fun. Is this Brazilian music?
Zac: Yes, it is.
Mina: Nice!
Conversation 3
Elena: What's your house like?
Kay: It's a new house. I like it.
Elena: What's your room like?
Kay: It's small. But I like it. It's quiet.
Elena: What color is it?
Kay: Pink. I love pink.

Track ▶76

Unit 1, page 77, Exercise 4

1
Lara: Where are you from, Diego?
2
Mina: Is this Brazilian music?
3
Elena: What's your house like?
4
Elena: What's your room like?
5
Elena: What color is it?

Track ▶77

Unit 2, page 86, Exercise 2, Exercise 3, Exercise 4, and Exercise 7

Mr. J: Hello and welcome to the Movie Quiz Show. My name is Mister J. Today we have Alan and Jill with us.
Alan: Hi, I'm Alan.
Jill: Hello. I'm Jill.
Mr. J: I have pictures of people from movies here. Ready? Picture number one. Whose ears are these? They're big. Here's some help. His teeth are horrible.
Jill: I think it's Gandalf from The Lord of the Rings.
Mr. J: No, that's wrong. Look at the ears. Those ears aren't his. Gandalf doesn't have big ears. Alan – do you have any ideas?
Alan: Is it Gollum from The Lord of the Rings?
Mr. J: Correct.
Picture number two. He's big and green, and his ears are long.
Jill: That's easy. It's Shrek. He has ears like that.
Mr. J: That's right.
Picture number three, who's this? He has a big head and body, and black eyes. He loves Jackie Chan.
Alan: Is it Master Shifu from Kung Fu Panda?
Mr. J: Sorry, but that's the wrong answer.
Jill: I think it's another panda – Po, the Kung Fu Panda?
Mr. J: You're absolutely right.
Picture number four. This person has long white hair.
Jill: That's Gandalf, right?
Mr. J: Very good, Jill! The winner is Jill. You win tickets to the new Spider-Man movie. Enjoy!

Track ▶78

Unit 2, page 86, Exercise 8

You see me in the movie Shrek. I have long ears, a big nose, four legs, and ... hee-haw ... no feet. Who am I?

Track ▶79

Unit 2, page 89, Exercise 1b

Make a call
Can I speak to ... ?
Is this ... ?
Is ... there?
Can he call me, please?
Can she call me, please?
Answer a call
Can you spell that, please?
Sorry, can you repeat that?
Sorry, I don't understand.
You have the wrong number.
Bye.
Goodbye.

Track ▶80

Unit 2, page 89, Exercise 2 and Exercise 4

Conversation 1
Mrs. Logan: Hello.
Lara: This is Lara Hardy. Is Kim there?
Mrs. Logan: No, she isn't, Lara. Sorry, she's out.
Lara: Can you ask her to call me, please?
Mrs. Logan: Sure. Bye, Lara.
Conversation 2
Mario: Good morning, Internet Answers. This is Mario.
John: Hello. This is John Phipps, and I have a problem with my internet.
Mario: OK, Mr. Phipps. How do you spell your name?
John: P-H-I-P-P-S.
Mario: And your telephone number?
John: 210-769-1264.
Mario: Sorry, can you repeat that?
John: 210-769-1264.
Mario: OK. Now what is the problem?

Conversation 3

Jess: Hello.

Lee: Kung hei fat choi.

Jess: Sorry, I don't understand. You have the wrong number.

Lee: No! It's me, Lee! Hi, Jess. It means "Happy New Year" in Chinese.

Jess: Oh, Lee! Thanks! Happy New Year to you too!

Track 81

Unit 2, page 89, Exercise 5

1

Lara: This is Lara Hardy. Is Kim there?

2

Mrs. Logan: Sorry, she's out.

3

Lara: Can you ask her to call me, please?

4

Mrs. Logan: Sure. Bye, Lara.

5

Mario: How do you spell your name?

6

Mario: Sorry, can you repeat that?

7

Jess: Sorry, I don't understand.

8

Jess: You have the wrong number.

Track 82

Unit 3, page 98, Exercise 2 and Exercise 3

Son: na-na-na-la-la ...

Mom: Shhh, stop it! You're so noisy!

Son: But we're on vacation, it's our new hotel room, and I'm happy.

Mom: OK, me too, but come on. Open the door. Let's go in ...

Son: What's this? Hmm ... Of course there's a bed, but it's very small, and there aren't any chairs.

Mom: And come here. Look! You can't see anything out of the window. There's just a wall.

Son: There's a light here ... but it doesn't work!

Mom: Aahh! There's a mouse on the floor over there under the table!

Son: Is there really a mouse?

Mom: I'm sorry, dear. Let's forget about this room. It's horrible. Let's go.

Track 83

Unit 3, page 98, Exercise 5b

1

Son: Of course there's a bed.

2

Son: There aren't any chairs.

3

Son: There's a light here.

4

Son: Is there really a mouse?

5

Mom: I'm sorry.

6

Mom: Let's forget about this room.

Track 84

Unit 3, page 100, Exercise 5

There's a mouse in my house.
But of course there isn't a horse.
There are mice, and they're nice, but there aren't any rabbits.
There's my dad – that's not bad, and there's my mom, and then there are some dogs, and a cat, and that's that!

Track 85

Unit 3, page 101, Exercise 1c

Ask for something

Can I have a ... , please?
Can I have some ... , please?
Excuse me. Can I borrow your ... ?

Give something

Here you are.

React

Yes, of course.
Sure.
You're welcome.
Thanks.
No, sorry.

Track 86

Unit 3, page 101, Exercise 2

Conversation 1

Rob: Ben, can I borrow your bike?

Ben: No, sorry. It's mine.

Rob: Please, Ben. Only for 30 minutes. Mom wants some milk from the store.

Ben: OK, but be careful with it.

Conversation 2

Mary: Mom? Can I have some money, please?

Mom: What for?

Mary: School lunch.

Mom: Yes, of course. Here you are.

Mary: Thanks.

Mom: You're welcome, Mary.

Conversation 3

Kate: Excuse me. Can I borrow your pen for a minute?

Dave: Sure. Here you are.

Kate: Thanks.

Dave: You're welcome. Hey, that's a cool phone!

Kate: Yeah. It's new.

Track 87

Unit 3, page 101, Exercise 3

Conversation 1

Rob: Ben, can I borrow your bike?

Ben: No, sorry. It's mine.

Conversation 2

Mary: Mom? Can I have some money, please?

Mom: Yes, of course. Here you are.

Mary: Thanks.

Mom: You're welcome, Mary.

Conversation 3

Kate: Excuse me. Can I borrow your pen for a minute?

Dave: Sure. Here you are.

Kate: Thanks.

Dave: You're welcome.

Track 88

Unit 3, page 103, Exercise 2a

Harriet: I prepare my clothes for school at night, but I don't finish my homework before bed. In the morning I don't have my lunch, so I have to make it quickly. I pack my bag really fast too. I know where my keys are. I always put them in my backpack before bed. I run to take the bus. Then I finish my homework on my way to school.

Track 89

Unit 4, page 110, Exercise 2 and Exercise 3

Tina: Welcome to *Tune In*, your Friday night music radio show with me, Tina Tee. Today we're out on the street talking to young people about their favorite music.

Tina: Hello, what's your name?

Dwayne: I'm Dwayne.

Tina: Hi, Dwayne. What music do you listen to?

Dwayne: I like hip hop.

Tina: And can you play an instrument or sing?

Dwayne: I can't play an instrument, but I can sing. I write songs. I write poems too.

Tina: That's great. Thanks. Good luck with it.

Tina: Hi. What's your name?

Yola: Yola.

Tina: So, what kind of music do you like?

Yola: I like traditional music.

Tina: Why do you like it?

Yola: The old songs are different. I think most pop is the same – boring.

Tina: Are you a good singer?

Yola: No. I can't sing, but I can play the guitar. I'm in a group called Harmony.

Tina: Do you play in concerts?

Yola: Yes. We sometimes play at school concerts.

Tina: Cool.

Tina: Excuse me. What's your name?

Leo: I'm Leo Jones.

Tina: Leo, are you musical?

Leo: Not really. I listen to a lot of music, and I play a little guitar.

Tina: What do you listen to?

Leo: I like old rock. Led Zeppelin, Pink Floyd – stuff like that.

Tina: What about new groups?

Leo: Yeah. I listen to them and go to concerts, but I really like old songs.

Tina: Thanks, Leo.

Track 90

Unit 4, page 113, Exercise 2

1 It's eleven o'clock.
2 It's a quarter to seven.
3 It's five to four.
4 It's four thirty.
5 It's ten to twelve.
6 It's twenty to nine.
7 It's ten after four.
8 It's a quarter to five.

Track 91

Unit 4, page 113, Exercise 3

1 It's a quarter to twelve.
2 It's ten to eleven.
3 It's eight thirty.
4 It's ten after nine.

Track 92

Unit 4, page 113, Exercise 4

Conversation 1

Jo: What time is it?
Mom: It's ten after eight.
Jo: Oh, no! We're late. The concert starts at a quarter after eight.
Mom: Relax. The concert is at eight thirty. We have time.

Conversation 2

Dan: What time's the movie?
Jo: It's at a quarter to nine.
Dan: Great. Let's go.

Conversation 3

Jo: Mom, what time is it now?
Mom: It's a quarter after one.
Jo: I have basketball practice at two o'clock.
Mom: OK. Have some lunch, and we can leave at ten to two. There's time.

Track 93

Unit 4, page 113, Exercise 5b

Ask the time

What time is it?
What time's the ... ?

Say the time

It's ... o'clock.
It's ten after ...
It's ten to ...
It's a quarter after ...
It's a quarter to ...
It's at ...

Track 94

Unit 4, page 113, Exercise 6

Conversation 1

Jo: What time is it?
Mom: It's ten after eight.
Jo: Oh, no! We're late. The concert starts at a quarter after eight.
Mom: Relax. The concert is at eight thirty. We have time.

Conversation 2

Dan: What time's the movie?
Jo: It's at a quarter to nine.
Dan: Great. Let's go.

Conversation 3

Jo: Mom, what time is it now?
Mom: It's a quarter after one.
Jo: I have basketball practice at two o'clock.
Mom: OK. Have some lunch, and we can leave at ten to two. There's time.

Track 95

Unit 4, page 115, Exercise 4

Teacher: Your homework is to write an essay on the history of movies. Use your book to help. Read Unit 6 and use the internet to find information. Write your essay in your notebook. You have one week. Write your essay by Tuesday, October 12.

WORKBOOK ANSWER KEY

Starter Unit

VOCABULARY 1

Page 66

1 **1** *e* **2** b **3** a **4** d **5** h **6** c **7** f **8** g
2 **1** *purple* **2** pink
3 **a** *one* **b** two **c** four **d** six **e** eight **f** twenty **g** twelve **h** fourteen **i** five **j** eighteen **k** nine **l** five **m** sixteen **n** ten **o** seventeen

GRAMMAR 1

Page 67

1 **1** *her* **2** my **3** your **4** their **5** They **6** Our **7** his
2 **1** *My* **2** I **3** My **4** My **5** She **6** Her **7** She **8** We **9** We **10** Our
3 **1** *It's* **2** Its **3** its **4** It's **5** its
4 **1** *b* **2** a **3** c **4** a **5** a **6** c **7** c **8** b
5 **1** *is* **2** are **3** are **4** is **5** is **6** am

VOCABULARY 2

Page 68

1a **1** April, August **2** January, June, July **3** March, May **4** *September,* October, November, December **5** February
1b **1** April = 30 days, August = 31 days **2** January = 31 days, June = 30 days, July = 31 days **3** March = 31 days, May = 31 days **4** September = *30* days, October = 31 days, November = 30 days, December = 31 days **5** February = 28/29 days
2 18 = *Sunday*, 19 = Monday, 20 = Tuesday, 21 = Wednesday, 22 = Thursday, 23 = Friday, 24 = Saturday
3a **1** *18* **2** 12 **3** 30 **4** 40 **5** 19 **6** 17 **7** 60 **8** 5
3b **1** *eighteen, eight* **2** twelve, twenty **3** three, thirty **4** four, forty **5** nineteen, nine
6 seventeen, seven **7** six, sixty **8** five, fifteen
4 **1** *35* **2** 21 **3** 56 **4** 83 **5** 97 **6** 74 **7** 49 **8** 62
5 **1** Name: Lucas Johnson; Phone number: 555-062-8397; Age: 13; Birthday: December 23; Address: 20 Sun Street, Miami, USA

GRAMMAR 2

Page 69

1a **1** *What color is it?* **2** How old is it? **3** Where is it now? **4** Is it a new phone? **5** Is it good?
1b **a** 3 **b** *1* **c** 4 **d** 2 **e** 5
2a **1** *Are* **2** Is **3** Are **4** Am **5** Is **6** Are **7** Is
2b **a** *1* **b** 4 **c** 6 **d** 7 **e** 2 **f** 3 **g** 5
3 **1** *Are you Carol? Yes, I am.*
2 Is he your teacher? / No, he isn't. / No, he's not.
3 Are we all here? / Yes, we are.
4 Are they good friends? / No, they're not. / No, they aren't.
5 Are you in the same class? / No, we're not. / No, we aren't.
6 Is it a good party? / Yes, it is.
7 Is she OK? / Yes, she is.
8 Am I on your team? / No, you're not. / No, you aren't.
4a **1** *Who* **2** Where **3** What **4** When **5** How **6** Where **7** What
4b **a** *1* **b** 5 **c** 6 **d** 2 **e** 4 **f** 3 **g** 7

Unit 1

VOCABULARY 1

Page 70

1 **1** *phone* **2** sunglasses **3** T-shirt **4** backpack **5** bike **6** laptop **7** soccer ball **8** game console
2 **1** *NOTEBOOK* **2** JEANS **3** ICE CREAM **4** PHONE **5** SANDWICH **6** WEBSITE **7** CAR

X	I	C	E	O	W	O	R	G	W
P	S	A	N	D	W	I	C	H	E
H	N	E	C	X	E	O	S	O	B
O	J	E	A	N	S	T	R	V	S
N	E	L	R	B	U	K	E	P	I
E	Q	R	E	Y	T	I	E	N	T
I	C	E	C	R	E	A	M	E	E
N	O	T	E	B	O	O	K	I	D

3 **1** *T-shirt* **2** soccer ball **3** jeans **4** ice-cream cone **6** bikes
4 **1** *e* **2** d **3** a **4** b **5** f **6** c

READING

Page 71

1 **1** *g* **2** a **3** b **4** d **5** c **6** e **7** f **8** h
2 **1** *hotel* **2** bus **3** email **4** television **5** café **6** pizza
3 **Transportation:** metro, bus, taxi **Food:** pizza, salad(s) **Places:** *hotel*, museum, café
4 Suggested answers: bus, stop, salads, soccer, television, WOW. (Any may be relevant.)
5 **1** *transportation* **2** taxi **3** café **4** Museum **5** aquarium **6** room **7** television **8** Wi-Fi **9** park **10** movies

GRAMMAR 1

Page 72

1a **1** *names* **2** buses **3** classes **4** lunches **5** boxes **6** cities **7** days
1b **1** ✓ **3** ✓ **5** ✓
2 **1** *a* **2** an **3** an **4** a **5** a **6** a
3 **1** – **2** – **3** the **4** – **5** the **6** the
4 **1** *a* **2** b **3** c **4** c **5** c **6** b **7** b

Page 73

5 **1** *lessons* **2** buses **3** cities **4** people **5** games **6** classes
6 **1** *children* **2** babies **3** girls **4** months **5** men **6** women **7** people
7 **1** *A, (-)*
2 A, (-)
3 (-), a
4 An, (-), a

LISTENING

Page 74

1 Students' own answers
2 **coffee:** Brazil **cars:** Italy, Germany, Japan **computers:** Japan, Germany **clothes:** Japan, Italy
3 **Italy:** *sports cars*, clothes, risotto **Brazil:** famous dances, coffee, bananas **Germany:** computers, cars **Japan:** cars, computers, clothes
4 **1** *Italian* **2** Brazilian **3** German **4** Japanese
5 **1** *Turkey* **2** English **3** China
6 **1** *Turkish* **2** England **3** Chinese
7 **1** *Where's it from?*
2 What's on the label?
3 I don't know.
4 It says "made in China."

VOCABULARY 2

Page 75

1 **1** *Brazil* **2** Germany **3** Italy **4** Japan **5** South Africa **6** Turkey **7** United States
2 **1** *Italian* **2** South African **3** Turkish **4** German **5** American **6** Japanese
3 **1** *Brazil* **2** South Africa **3** Italy **4** Japanese **5** American **6** Germans **7** Turkish

Words & Beyond

4a **1** *d* **2** c **3** a **4** f **5** b **6** e
4b **1** *boring* **2** interesting **3** new **4** different **5** big **6** old
5 **1** *glass* **2** sandwich **3** story **4** article **5** city **6** game
6 **1** *tourists* **2** vacations **3** visit **4** cities **5** museums **6** stay **7** hotels

GRAMMAR 2

Page 76

1 **1** *this* **2** that **3** these **4** those
2 **1** *'s* **2** is/'s **3** are **4** are **5** Are **6** are
3 **1** *that* **2** Those **3** that **4** This **5** these
4a **1** *this* **2** those **3** those **4** that **5** that **6** this **7** those **8** these
4b **a** *2* **b** 8 **c** 7 **d** 4 **e** 1 **f** 6 **g** 5 **h** 3
5 **1** *Who is that?*
2 What are those things?
3 Why is this movie so boring?
4 What are these things called?
5 Where's this place on the map?
6 How old is that house?

SPEAKING

Page 77

1a **1** *is* **2** like **3** it **4** It's **5** They **6** really **7** are
2 **1** *Brazil* **2** Colombia **3** party **4** pink
3 **1** *e* **2** f **3** b **4** c **5** d **6** a

WRITING

Page 78

1 **1** *adjective* **2** noun **3** adjective
2 **1** *This is* **2** African **3** really big **4** favorite animal **5** very happy **6** a good

3a **1** *b* **2** a **3** c **4** f **5** d **6** e
3b **1** *funny* **2** great, cool **3** favorite, blue, nice **4** black, fast **5** old, noisy
6 Japanese
4 **1** *This is my new bike.*
2 These clothes are really nice. / These are really nice clothes.
3 This is my French pen pal, Vanessa.
4 My house isn't very big.
5 My best friend is really funny.

SCHOOL SKILLS
Page 79
1 **1** *a* **2** g **3** f **4** c **5** b **6** e **7** d
2 **1** *good* **2** respect **3** teacher
4 students **5** all **6** learn
3 **1** *b* **2** c **3** a **4** f **5** e **6** d

VOCABULARY REVIEW 1
Page 80
1 **1** *red* **2** blue **3** orange **4** pink
5 brown **6** white **7** yellow **8** green
2 **1** *b* **2** e **3** a **4** c **5** g **6** d **7** f
3 **1** *b* **2** a **3** c **4** a **5** b **6** c **7** a **8** c

GRAMMAR REVIEW 1
Page 81
1a **1** *Where* **2** Who **3** Where **4** Where
5 What **6** When **7** How
1b **a** *1* **b** 5 **c** 7 **d** 3 **e** 2 **f** 4 **g** 6
2a **1** *Is, your* **2** Are, – **3** Is, you **4** Are, her **5** Are **6** Is, your
2b **1** *No, it isn't.* **2** Yes, I am. **3** No, it isn't. **4** Yes, they are. **5** No, we aren't.
6 Yes, it is.
3 **1** *a* **2** is **3** This **4** our **5** – **6** an **7** are
8 a
4 **1** *buses* **2** classes **3** friends
4 lunches **5** activities **6** classmates
7 days

Unit 2

VOCABULARY 1
Page 82
1 **1** *different* **2** new **3** horrible **4** good
5 same **6** quiet **7** bad **8** noisy **9** young
10 similar **11** nice

D	N	G	Q	B	Z	F	E	S
N	I	E	O	H	A	L	Y	I
O	S	F	W	O	B	D	O	M
I	A	R	F	I	D	L	U	I
S	M	M	R	E	Y	G	N	L
Y	E	R	W	U	R	E	G	A
J	O	R	Q	U	I	E	T	R
H	N	I	C	E	G	M	N	S
Z	K	W	Z	E	I	F	F	T

2 same
3 **1** young **2** new
4 **1** *quiet* **2** horrible **3** new **4** good
5 same **6** nice

5 **Male:** *dad*, father, grandpa, brother
Female: grandma, mother, sister, mom
6 **1** Luis **2** Paula **3** Omar **4** Tina
5 Marcos **6** *Sara*
7 **1** *T* **2** F **3** F **4** T **5** T **6** T

READING
Page 83
1 **1** *f* **2** h **3** g **4** c **5** d **6** b **7** a **8** e **9** i
10 j
2 **1** Anna **2** Lili **3** Dana
3 **1** *b* **2** a **3** f **4** e **5** h **6** i **7** c **8** j **9** d
10 g
4 **a** 4 **b** 2 **c** 5 **d** 8 **e** 7 **f** *1* **g** 3 **h** 6

GRAMMAR 1
Page 84
1 **1** *have* **2** has **3** don't **4** doesn't **5** Do
6 Does **7** do **8** doesn't
2 **1** *don't* **2** don't **3** don't **4** has
5 doesn't **6** don't **7** have **8** have
3a **1** *Does Clara have a brother?*
2 Does Mike have a sister?
3 Does Clara have a sister?
4 Does Mike have a brother?
5 Do Clara and Mike have laptops?
6 Do they have tablets?
7 Does Clara have a game console?
3b **1** *No, she doesn't.* **2** Yes, he does.
3 Yes, she does. **4** No, he doesn't.
5 No, they don't. **6** Yes, they do. **7** Yes, she does.

Page 85
4 **1** *Do you have a good movie we can watch?*
2 No, I don't.
3 Do you have a DVD?
4 I have a DVD of *How to Train Your Dragon*.
5 I don't have that.
6 Do you have anything to eat?
7 I have pizza.
5 **1** *Does John have a problem with math? Yes, he does.*
2 Do Kate and Mary have the same last name? Yes, they do.
3 Does Anna have a big house? Yes, she does.
4 Do you have a favorite game? No, I don't.
5 Do we have a problem here? No, we don't.
6 Do I have the correct answers? No, I don't.
6 **1** *Do you have your T-shirts?*
2 *Yes, I do.*
3 Do you have your sunglasses?
4 No, I don't.
5 Does the hotel have big rooms?
6 Yes, it does.
7 Does the hotel have a swimming pool?
8 No, it doesn't.
9 Does your sister have my phone?
10 Yes, she does.
11 Does she have my camera too?
12 No, she doesn't.

LISTENING
Page 86
1 **a** 5 **b** 4 **c** 2 **d** 3 **e** 1
2 **1** *Mr. J* **2** Mr. J **3** Jill **4** Mr. J **5** Alan
6 Mr. J **7** Mr. J **8** Jill **9** Mr. J **10** Mr. J
11 Jill **12** Mr. J
4 Gandalf ✓ Gollum ✓ Po ✓ Shrek ✓
5 **1** *Gollum* **2** Shrek **3** Po **4** Gandalf
6 c
8 d

VOCABULARY 2
Page 87
1 **1** *nose* **2** eyes **3** mouth **4** ears
5 legs **6** teeth
2 **1** *b* **2** c **3** f **4** e **5** d **6** a
3 **1** *head* **2** eyes **3** feet **4** arms
5 mouth **6** nose

Words & Beyond
4 **1** *time* **2** smart **3** morning **4** spell
5 park **6** present
5 **1** *camera* **2** Smile **3** text message
4 contact list **5** laptop **6** wrong number

GRAMMAR 2
Page 88
1 **1** *mom's* **2** parents' **3** is that
2 **1** *mine* **2** yours **3** his **4** hers **5** ours
6 theirs
3a **1** *Whose room is this?*
2 Whose pens are these?
3 Whose phone is this?
4 Whose jeans are these?
5 Whose bike is this?
6 Whose books are these?
3b **1** *It's Matt's.* **2** They're Matt's. **3** It's Alicia's. **4** They're Matt's. **5** It's Alicia's.
6 They're Alicia's.
4 **1** a ✓, b *parents'* **2** a ✓, b girls'
3 a grandpa's, b ✓ **4** a neighbor's / neighbors', b ✓ **5** a team's, b ✓ **6** a ✓, b students'
5 **1** *dad's* **2** mine **3** mom's **4** parents'
5 sister's **6** Hers
6 **1** *Whose dad is he? He's Juanita's.*
2 Whose grandchildren are they? They're mine.
3 Whose brother is he? He's Mario's.
4 Whose mother is she? She's ours.
5 Whose child is this? He's/she's theirs.
6 Whose parents are they? They're Kim's.

SPEAKING
Page 89
1a **1** speak to **2** call **3** spell **4** repeat
5 understand **6** have
2 **1** c **2** b **3** a
3 **1** *there* **2** Sorry **3** Can **4** please
5 Bye **6** do **7** can **8** Hello **9** understand
10 number
6 Students' own answers

WRITING
Page 90
1 **1** letter **2** possessive
2 **1** *Shakira's* **2** She's **3** I'm **4** sister's
5 don't **6** Dad's **7** It's
3 Picture a (Jack Sparrow)
4 Picture b

SCHOOL SKILLS
Page 91
1 **1** *hello* **2** family **3** nice **4** favorite
5 phone
2 **1** *I like your bag.*
2 Do you have brothers and sisters?
3 Where do you live?
4 Who's your favorite singer?
5 Are you on a sports team?
6 Hi, I'm Angie.
3 **1** *isn't* **2** are **3** Talk **4** new
4 **1** ✓ **2** ✓ **3** ✗ **4** ✓ **5** ✓ **6** ✗

VOCABULARY REVIEW 1&2
Page 92
1 **1** *h* **2** a **3** d **4** g **5** f **6** c **7** e **8** b
2 **1** *b* **2** a **3** c **4** a **5** a **6** b
3 **1** *mom* **2** me **3** sister **4** child **5** home
6 room **7** street **8** park **9** school
4 *ice cream*, pen, eye, ear, bike, street
5

A	S	C	H	I	L	D
S	C	H	O	O	L	E
I	A	T	M	M	O	M
S	T	R	E	E	T	B
T	P	A	R	K	Y	I
E	Y	E	A	R	E	K
R	O	O	M	O	Y	E

GRAMMAR REVIEW 1&2
Page 93
1 **1** *there* **2** their **3** Who's **4** Whose
5 Who's **6** their **7** Whose
2 **1** *am* **2** is **3** are **4** has **5** This
6 These **7** is
3 **1** *b* **2** c **3** b **4** c **5** a **6** c **7** a **8** b
4a **1** *Are* **2** Does **3** Do **4** Is **5** What
6 Where **7** When **8** What
4b **a** *2* **b** 7 **c** 4 **d** 3 **e** 8 **f** 5 **g** 1 **h** 6

Unit 3

VOCABULARY 1
Page 94
1 **1** *eyes* **2** ears **3** legs **4** feet **5** arms
6 face **7** mouth **8** nose **9** teeth

L	E	G	S	H	H	X	C
N	G	X	T	T	Q	M	L
N	E	U	E	N	I	D	W
D	O	E	F	A	I	V	V
M	T	S	Y	A	R	M	S
H	Y	S	E	E	C	S	T
W	J	F	X	C	S	E	X
J	E	F	E	E	T	M	N

2 **1** *b* **2** a **3** f **4** g **5** e **6** d **7** c
3 **1** *horse* **2** chicken **3** hamster **4** turtle
5 bird **6** fish
4 **1** *fish* **2** mice **3** horse **4** chickens
5 cats **6** dog **7** mice

READING
Page 95
1 **1** cat **2** special kitten milk
2 **1** *e* **2** c **3** b **4** d **5** a **6** f
3 **1** *F* **2** T **3** F **4** F **5** F **6** T

GRAMMAR 1
Page 96
1 **1** *Close* **2** Don't **3** me **4** you **5** him
6 her **7** us **8** them
2 **1** *them* **2** her **3** us **4** him **5** me **6** it
3 **1** *Come in* **2** Sit in **3** eat **4** Don't
5 Go **6** Don't **7** Write
4 **1** *b* **2** d **3** a **4** c **5** f **6** e
5a **1** *b* **2** a **3** d **4** c **5** f **6** e
5b **1** *b* **2** d **3** a **4** c

Page 97
6 **1** *Give* **2** Take **3** Don't say **4** Play
5 Don't keep **6** Be
7 **1** *it* **2** me **3** it **4** them **5** him **6** her
7 them **8** us
8 **1** *d* **2** f **3** e **4** a **5** b **6** c
9a **1** *Turn right here.* **2** Don't park here.
3 Don't drive fast here. **4** Don't walk your dog here. **5** Cross the street here.
6 Call for help here. **7** Wait for the bus here. **8** Ask questions here.
9b **a** 8 **b** 3 **c** 2 **d** *1* **e** 4 **f** 7 **g** 6 **h** 5

LISTENING
Page 98
1 **2** ✓ **4** ✓ **5** ✓
2 **1** *two* **2** no **3** a mouse **4** no
3 **1** ✓ **3** ✓ **4** ✓ **5** ✓ **6** ✓ **7** ✓ **8** ✓
4 **1** *F* **2** T **3** F **4** F **5** F **6** T
5a **1** *course* **2** There aren't **3** There's
4 Is there **5** sorry **6** forget

VOCABULARY 2
Page 99
1 **1** *picture* **2** window **3** bed **4** chair
5 desk **6** wall
2 **1** *b* **2** f **3** a **4** e **5** d **6** c
3 **1** *floor* **2** chair **3** bed

Words & Beyond
4a **1** e **2** a **3** b **4** d **5** c
4b **1** *easy* **2** lies down **3** quiet **4** wait
5 noisy **6** difficult **7** go **8** stands up
9 nice
5 **1** *perfect* **2** grass **3** shake **4** wait
5 cross **6** neighbor

GRAMMAR 2
Page 100
1 **1** *is* **2** are **3** isn't **4** aren't **5** Is **6** is
7 isn't **8** Are **9** are **10** aren't
2 **1** *There's* **2** isn't **3** are **4** aren't
5 There's **6** there's **7** There are **8** isn't
3a **1** *any* **2** any **3** a **4** a **5** any **6** any
3b **1** *there aren't* **2** there are **3** there is
4 there isn't **5** there aren't **6** there are
4 **1** *There's* **2** there isn't **3** There are
4 there aren't **5** There's **6** there's
7 there are
6 **1** *Is there a clock? No, there isn't.*
2 Are there any chairs? Yes, there are.
3 Are there any students? No, there aren't.
4 Are there any books? Yes, there are.
5 Is there a dog? No, there isn't.
6 Is there a cat? No, there isn't.
7 **1** *Are there big windows in the room?*
2 *Yes, there are.*
3 Is there a computer in the room?
4 No, there isn't.
5 Is there free Wi-Fi?
6 Yes, there is.
7 Is there a restaurant at the hotel?
8 Yes, there is.
9 Are there parks near the hotel?
10 No, there aren't.

SPEAKING
Page 101
1a **1** *please* **2** course **3** are **4** welcome
5 borrow **6** sorry
1b **1** *please* **2** borrow **3** are **4** course
5 welcome **6** sorry
2 **1** ✓ **3** ✓ **5** ✓
4 Students' own answers

WRITING
Page 102
1 **1** *Write* **2** Use **3** Don't write
2 **2** ✓
3 **1** ✓
4 Suggested answer: James. I'm at work. Please take Max for a walk. Thanks, Dad
5 **1** a dog (Tim's dog) **2** at the office (at work) **3** piano lesson (Harry's piano lesson) **4** at work **5** the soccer game
6 pasta

SCHOOL SKILLS
Page 103

1 1 *bed* **2** good **3** quickly
2a 1 *T* **2** F **3** T **4** F **5** F
2b Suggested answer: No, she isn't.
3 1 *b* **2** b **3** b **4** a **5** a **6** b

VOCABULARY REVIEW 1–3
Page 104

1 1 *a* **2** b **3** c **4** b **5** a **6** c **7** b **8** a **9** c
2 1 *eye* **2** nose **3** ear **4** head **5** mouth **6** teeth
3 1 *EYE* **2** EAR **3** MOUTH **4** HEAD **5** TEETH **6** LEG **7** ARM **8** FACE

F	P	C	Q	H	H
A	E	H	T	T	L
C	V	U	E	Y	E
E	O	E	E	A	R
M	T	A	R	M	D
L	E	G	D	C	C

4 1 *Brazilian* **2** Turkey **3** Italian **4** teeth **5** horses **6** bird

GRAMMAR REVIEW 1–3
Page 105

1 1 *have* **2** don't **3** There **4** us **5** sisters **6** don't **7** the **8** my
2a 1 *Do* **2** Are **3** Does **4** Do **5** Does **6** Is **7** Do
2b a 2 **b** 1/4 **c** 6 **d** 7 **e** 1/4 **f** 3 **g** 5
3 1 *b* **2** a **3** b **4** a **5** c **6** b
4 1 *b* **2** a **3** c **4** b **5** a **6** c **7** c **8** a

Unit 4

VOCABULARY 1
Page 106

1 1 soccer **2** shopping **3** internet **4** bike **5** friends **6** movies **7** book **8** music
2 1 *f* **2** a **3** b **4** c **5** d **6** e
3 1 *video* **2** bike **3** television **4** music **5** internet **6** friends
4 1 *bikes* **2** internet **3** friends **4** book **5** soccer **6** movies
5a 1 *watch* **2** go **3** read **4** meet **5** go **6** go **7** ride **8** listen
5b 1 ✓ **2** ✓ **3** ✓ **4** ✗ **5** ✗ **6** ✓ **7** ✓

READING
Page 107

1 1 ✓
2 1 *F* **2** F **3** T
3 1 *b* **2** b **3** b **4** a **5** a

GRAMMAR 1
Page 108

1 1 *can* **2** can't **3** Can **4** can **5** can't
2 1 *c* **2** a **3** b **4** c **5** a **6** b **7** c
3a 1 *Can babies walk?*
2 Can dogs swim?
3 Can chickens make eggs?
4 Can Ronaldo play soccer?
5 Can Lady Gaga sing?
6 Can a fish talk?
7 Can deaf people hear?
8 Can you play this sport?
3b 1 *No, they can't.* **2** Yes, they can. **3** Yes, they can. **4** Yes, he can. **5** Yes, she can. **6** No, it can't. **7** No, they can't **8** Yes, I can. / No, I can't. (Students' own answers)

Page 109

4 1 *can* **2** can **3** can't **4** can **5** can **6** Can **7** can't **8** can
5 1 *can speak Japanese.*
2 can ride a bike.
3 can't cook.
4 can play tennis.
5 can't speak Japanese.
6 can ride a bike.
7 can't cook.
8 can't play tennis.
6 Students' own answers
7 1 *You can't write notes to your friends.*
2 You can ask the/your/a teacher questions.
3 You can't do homework for other subjects.
4 You can't eat lunch.
5 You can't use your/a/the phone.
6 You can answer your/the teacher's questions.
7 You can't shout at (your) classmates.
8 You can talk to a/your partner.

LISTENING
Page 110

1 Students' own answers
2 1 *c* **2** a **3** b
3 1 *Y & L* **2** D **3** Y **4** Y & L **5** D **6** Y
4 1 *What music do you listen to?*
2 Can you play an instrument?
3 What kind of music do you like?
4 Are you a good singer?
5 Are you musical?
6 What about new groups?
5 1 *I listen to hip-hop.* **2** Yes, I can. **3** I like traditional music. **4** No, I'm not. **5** Yes, I am. **6** I like them.

VOCABULARY 2
Page 111

1 1 *HIP-HOP* **2** ROCK **3** LATIN **4** CLASSICAL **5** POP **6** GUITAR **7** VIOLIN **8** KEYBOARD **9** DRUMS **10** PIANO

D	H	C	P	W	T	N	N	L
R	R	I	K	O	I	X	A	G
U	O	Y	P	L	P	C	D	U
M	C	J	O	H	I	E	Z	I
S	K	I	B	S	O	R	D	T
O	V	G	S	I	M	P	X	A
G	L	A	T	I	N	T	I	R
C	L	P	I	A	N	O	S	O
C	K	E	Y	B	O	A	R	D

2 1 *b* **2** d **3** e **4** c **5** a
3 1 *keyboard* **2** violin **3** guitar **4** classical **5** pop **6** rock

Words & Beyond

4 1 *hearing aid* **2** blind **3** sign **4** deaf **5** dark **6** disability
5 1 *sing* **2** touch **3** pass **4** dance **5** play

GRAMMAR 2
Page 112

1 1 *play* **2** plays **3** does **4** watches **5** studies **6** has
2 1 *studies* **2** play **3** writes **4** makes **5** love **6** listen **7** practice **8** goes
3 1 *a* **2** b **3** c **4** b **5** c **6** b **7** a **8** c
4 1 *likes* **2** plays **3** sings **4** studies **5** practices **6** goes **7** teaches
5 1 *spends* **2** listens **3** writes **4** watches **5** tries **6** think **7** go

SPEAKING
Page 113

1 1 *b* **2** c **3** c **4** a **5** b **6** a **7** c **8** a
3 1 b **2** a **3** a **4** b
4 1 a ✓ **2** a ✓ **3** b ✓
5a 1 time **2** time **3** It's **4** It's **5** It's **6** It's **7** It's
7 Students' own answers

WRITING
Page 114

1 1 *b* **2** e **3** c **4** d **5** a
2 Hi Graciela,
It's great to hear from you. Your English is very good. It's fantastic that we can meet on Saturday. I think we can go out at night. Call me when you get to San Diego. My mom can pick you up at the Solana Beach bus station.
Love,
Carole
3 1 *Egypt* **2** Paris **3** Where **4** I **5** John **6** Thursday
4 1 *Hi Anna,*
2 It's great to hear from you again.
3 Well, I have my first concert on Saturday.

4 We sing traditional Spanish songs.
5 I'm a little nervous about it.
6 Best wishes,
7 Antonio

SCHOOL SKILLS

Page 115

1 **1** ✓ **3** ✓ **6** ✓
2 **1** c **2** b **3** a
3 ✓ *1* 2 4 5 6 7
4 **1** *essay* **2** history of movies **3** 6/six
4 notebook **5** Tuesday, October 12th

VOCABULARY REVIEW 1–4

Page 116

1 **1** *wastebasket* **2** apple **3** tourists
4 Smile **5** idea **6** wrong **7** chair
8 shake
2a **1** *EASY* **2** OLD **3** LIGHT **4** DARK
5 TALL **6** YOUNG **7** NOISY **8** NICE

N	O	I	S	Y	E
I	L	I	G	H	T
C	D	A	R	K	A
E	A	S	Y	E	L
Y	O	U	N	G	L

2b **1** *tall* **2** easy **3** dark **4** light **5** nice
6 old **7** young **8** noisy
3 **1** *b* **2** c **3** c **4** a **5** c **6** a **7** b **8** b

GRAMMAR REVIEW 1–4

Page 117

1 **1** *Do* **2** ✓ **3** ✓ **4** Do **5** have **6** ✓
7 has **8** have
2 **1** *are* **2** are **3** is **4** is **5** are **6** aren't
7 isn't **8** are
3 **1** *am* **2** can **3** do **4** we can **5** we
6 can
4 **1** *take* **2** put **3** ask **4** see **5** run **6** sit
7 dance
5 **1** *There's* **2** here **3** do **4** Help **5** come
6 love **7** is

Macmillan Education
4 Crinan Street
London N1 9XW
A division of Macmillan Publishers Limited

Companies and representatives throughout the world

ISBN 978-1-380-00781-0

Written by Anna Cole, David Corp, and Alexandra Hearn

Go Beyond First published 2016
First edition entitled *Beyond* published 2015

Designed by EMC Design Ltd.
Cover design by EMC Design Ltd.
DVD/CD/on-body design by Dynamo Studio, Co.

Full acknowledgements for illustrations and photographs in the facsimile pages can be found in the combined Student's Book/Workbook.

Printed and bound in China

2021 2020 2019 2018 2017
10 9 8 7 6 5 4 3 2 1